How to choose your A-levels

THIRD EDITION

David Cooper

How to choose your A-levels, third edition

This third edition published in 2000
by Trotman and Company Ltd
2 The Green, Richmond, Surrey TW9 1PL

© Trotman and Company Limited 2000

First edition published in 1995
Second edition published in 1996

British Library Cataloguing in Publication Data
A catalogue record for this book is available from the
British Library.

ISBN 1 900609 21 5

Typeset by Florence Production Ltd, Stoodleigh, Devon
Printed and bound in Great Britain
by Creative Print & Design (Wales) Ltd

Contents

About the author

David Cooper has worked in further education and taught A-level Biological Science for 21 years. He was responsible for A-level provision at Warrington Collegiate Institute for ten years and established the Warrington A-level Centre within the Institute. He has been an examiner and team leader for AQA A-level Biology and Human Biology since 1988 and is currently Director of Teaching and Learning at Askham Bryan College near York.

Introduction

The General Certificate of Education Advanced Level qualifications or A-levels remain by far the most popular, and many would argue the most valued, means by which students aged 17 or 18 can gain access to degree programmes and the world of Higher Education. They are widely perceived by employers as an understandable benchmark of educational achievement in contrast with a myriad of vocational qualifications, which can be difficult to evaluate and the titles and structures of which are subject to frequent change. For these reasons A-levels are frequently described as the *gold standard* of the British education system.

However, all in the garden is not rosy. A-level programmes were often narrow in their focus and taught over relatively few hours per week when compared with their European counterparts. The Advanced Supplementary or AS-level has been a complete flop, regarded by students and many teachers as being disproportionately large in terms of size and rigour when compared with its effectiveness as a means of gaining entry to university degree courses. By design, A-levels lack relevance to the world of work but it continued to be difficult to combine academic qualifications with those of a more vocational nature and the academic-vocational divide remained as a meaningless but very real barrier within our education system. The Key skills (see page 38), universally valued by both employers and university tutors, were not explicitly identified in A-level syllabuses and the narrow programmes mentioned previously would often preclude students from one or more of these essential areas of study. Finally, there was an excessive number of different syllabuses within the same subject offered by eight different examining boards. Whilst this could have been regarded as a desirable breadth of choice, that choice was not passed on to the learner as institutions generally offer one syllabus only in each subject. The number of different syllabuses in any one subject raised fears over quality control and suspicion that levels of difficulty varied and that the gold standard was devalued.

However, the times they are a changing. New A-levels are now offered in fewer specifications by fewer examination boards which also offer vocational qualifications. Key skills are embedded and explicitly sign-posted in all A-level specifications designed for the 2002 examinations and beyond. The majority of learners on A-level programmes now study the national key skills qualification alongside and within their A-level subjects.The General National Vocational qualifications, known as GNVQs, have been re-badged and re-engineered as Vocational A-levels. The changes allow easy combination with academic subjects and the qualifications have moved closer together in terms of size, methods of assessment and grading of achievement. Time will tell as to whether we have finally thrown a permanent bridge across the academic-vocational divide.

All A-level students now study the new AS-level as the first part of study towards the new A-level or as an end in itself. Again the jury is still out as to whether this will engineer the broadening of A-level programmes desired by government policy. The value students and teachers will place on breadth and diversity within A-level programmes is largely in the hands of University gate-keepers, rather than being a desirable goal for its own sake.

The new A-levels in both their academic and vocational guises described in the following pages have a consistency and simplicity of structure which enables ease of understanding. The new National Qualification Framework will create a world through which students can navigate their route through education with the confidence that the value of their learning is better understood by those who offer degree places and those who hand out jobs.

Section 1

The A-level system

A-levels: an overview

The Advanced Level examination is the flagship of our education programme for those aged between 16 and 18 in England, Wales and Northern Ireland. 'A-levels' enable those who wish to remain in school or college after the age of compulsory schooling to continue their education for another two years – either with the aim of going on to university or college to study for a degree or diploma, or with the aim of embarking on employment or professional or further vocational training.

A-levels have for the main part been considered to be *academic* in nature, with the exception of a few such as Business Studies and Media Studies that have elements with a more *vocational* theme. This will change from September 2000 when the education initiatives known collectively as *Curriculum 2000* introduce the concept of the *Vocational A-level*, which was developed from the GNVQ family of courses.

Academic or GCE A-levels develop intellectual skills rather than practical or vocational ones. They teach you how to ask questions about and analyse such matters as what caused the First World War; what happens to metals when they are subject to heat; why Shakespeare is believed to be our best dramatist; what causes inflation; how advertisements affect our judgement.

One significant feature of the A-level system – which sets it apart from its equivalents in almost every other country – is the wide variety of choice it offers. A glance at the table on pages 35–37 shows that there are over 65 subjects that you may study at A-level, from the traditional sciences and humanities to the more contemporary social sciences and some practical and applied subjects. There are also over 20 modern languages that may be taken at A-level.

As the table also shows, the choice is even wider than these numbers suggest. In most other countries there is just one examining authority for school examinations. In the UK there are five A-level examining bodies, each offering their own version of the more popular subjects; those with relatively few entrants are normally offered by one or two examining bodies. The design and content of A-level courses, called the *specification*, is validated by the *Qualifications and Curriculum Authority (QCA)*. In most subjects QCA lays down a number of subject criteria to which A-levels in that subject must conform. Summaries of the subject criteria are included in the final section of this book. However, the different examining bodies do enable choice through the provision of a number of styles and options for study, including the amount and type of coursework required by the qualification.

The Curriculum 2000 initiative was designed to introduce an element of breadth into A-level study. Prior to September 2000 students normally chose two, three or four A-level subjects that would be studied over two years to complete the qualifications. Whilst this system was the envy of many countries in terms of the *depth* of study it allowed, in the UK many were aware that the subject combinations studied were often too specialised and narrow, lacking the breadth that was desirable for general education at this level. From September 2000 students will be offered the *Advanced Subsidiary (AS) level* qualifications in the first year of the course and full-time students would normally study four or five subjects. The number of subjects would then reduce to two, three or four in the second year of the course (called *A2*), which would then be carried on to the full A-level. By August 2002 students will be offering a number of A-levels *plus* one or two AS-levels in different subjects as they take up places in higher education or employment.

There are few restrictions on the combination of subjects you may study. Some examining boards do not allow you to take two subjects where there is substantial overlap in the material studied, but their rules do not prevent you from concentrating on the sciences (Biology, Chemistry and Physics as a popular combination) or from taking three modern languages.

In practice, of course, your freedom to choose any subject and specification in any combination, is likely to be restricted by the administrative arrangements of the school or college where you are studying and by the fact that very few schools or colleges have facilities for teaching all the subjects set by all the examining boards.

All A-levels are composed of six elements, which may be referred to as *modules* or *units*. The first three units comprise the AS-level with the final three studied as A2. Units may be taken throughout the course in both January and June of the first and second years. This is known as the *modular route* and is ideal if you are not very good at storing up a large amount of learning and keeping it in mind for two whole years. Conversely many students improve in their ability over the duration of the course and may not be ready for assessment as early as January of the second year. For these students a *linear* course may be preferable, with all units being assessed at the end of the two years. A number of variations are possible. For example students may wish to take the three AS units together in the June of the first year, take one A2 unit in the January of year 2 and the final two A2 units in the June of year 2. Students who fail any unit assessment are allowed only one resit.

A-level examining boards

In the second half of the 1990s the six English A-level examining boards merged with a number of awarding bodies offering vocational qualifications to form three unitary awarding bodies: the Edexcel Foundation, the Assessment and Qualifications Alliance (AQA) and Oxford, Cambridge and RSA Examinations (OCR). These together with the Welsh Joint Education Committee (WJEC) and the Northern Ireland Council for the Curriculum, Examinations and Assessment (CCEA) form the five bodies offering A-level specifications in the United Kingdom.

The addresses of the five awarding bodies are:

AQA
Assessment & Qualifications Alliance
Stag Hill House, Guildford, Surrey GU2 7XJ
01483 506506
www.aqa.org.uk

CCEA
Northern Ireland Council for the Curriculum, Examinations and Assessment
Clarendon Dock, 29 Clarendon Rd, Belfast BT1 3BG
01232 261200
www.ccea.org.uk

EDEXCEL
The Edexcel Foundation
Stewart House, 32 Russell Square, London WC1B 5DN
020 7393 4500
www.edexcel.org.uk

OCR
Oxford, Cambridge and RSA Examinations
1 Hills Rd, Cambridge CB1 2EU
01223 553998
www.ocr.org.uk

WJEC
Welsh Joint Education Committee
245 Western Ave, Cardiff CF5 2YX
029 2026 5000
www.wjec.co.uk

Responsibilities of the boards

These include:

- developing syllabuses
- setting examination papers
- appointing examiners
- marking exam papers
- awarding grades and certificates
- liaising with schools and colleges.

QCA

Examining boards are independent bodies but they must work within guidelines laid down by the Department for Education and Employment via its agency known as the QCA. A-level specifications, standards and marking procedures are all subject to and controlled by the QCA.

A-LEVEL STATISTICS – PROVISIONAL A-LEVEL RESULTS, JUNE 1999

Joint council for general qualifications

Subject	Number Sat	% of Total No. Sat	Percentages by grade							
			A	B	C	D	E	N	U
Art and design subjects*	37385	4.8	23.6	21	24	17.4	9.3	3.6	1.1
Biology	56036	7.2	17.4	19.1	19.4	17.6	13.6	8	4.9
Business studies	37926	4.8	9.0	19.3	24.4	20.5	13.5	7.8	5.5
Chemistry	41727	5.3	24.5	21.6	18.8	14.8	10.6	6	3.7
Classical subjects*	5917	0.8	27.1	23.7	20.8	13.5	8.4	4	2.5
Computing	17145	2.2	8.7	13.6	20.3	22	17.6	9.8	8
Economics	18377	2.3	19.3	18.7	19.4	17.2	13.1	7.1	5.2
English*	90340	11.5	15.2	19.2	23.8	21.1	13.4	5.2	2.1
French	21072	2.7	23.2	20.4	20.1	16.4	11.3	5.7	2.9
General studies	85338	10.9	12.5	16.8	19.2	19.7	15.8	9.6	6.4
Geography	42181	5.4	16.3	22.4	23.6	19	11.1	5.3	2.3
German	9551	1.2	27.5	19.6	19	14.8	11.1	5.1	2.9
History	38482	4.9	16.8	20.1	21.5	18	11.5	6.6	5.5
Law	10703	1.4	11.4	13.6	16.6	17.8	14.8	11.2	14.5
Mathematics	69945	8.9	28.3	19	16.5	13.8	10.7	6.6	5.1
Media/Film/TV Studies*	14222	1.8	9.7	16.8	30	25.1	12.1	4.2	2.1
Music	6875	0.9	20.3	20.5	24.7	18.6	10.1	4.2	1.6

A-LEVEL STATISTICS (cont.)

Joint council for general qualifications

Subject	Number Sat	% of Total No. Sat	Percentages by grade						
			A	B	C	D	E	N	U
Physics	33880	4.3	24.1	20	18.8	15.3	11.3	6.6	3.9
Psychology	28737	3.7	11.9	17.8	20.6	18.3	14	10.1	7.3
Religious studies	8997	1.1	17.4	20.4	23.9	17.7	10.5	6.7	4.4
Sociology	24749	3.2	12.7	18.6	19.2	16.3	14.5	10.2	8.5
Spanish	5782	0.7	24.6	23.8	20.4	15.3	8.8	4	3.1
Sport/PE studies	15788	2.0	9.4	13	23.1	25.5	18.7	7.8	2.5
Technology subjects*	13727	1.8	13.6	14.8	24.7	23	14.3	6.3	3.3
Welsh	957	0.1	18.4	25.8	24	16.2	10.1	3.8	1.7
All Subjects	783692	100	17.5	19	21	18.3	12.7	6.9	4.5

*These titles cover a range of related subjects

A-level exam administration

Exam entries

Entries for A-levels are normally made through the institution where you are studying. If you are not attached to any institution then you should approach a school or college in your area that runs exams of the board for whose A-level syllabus you are preparing. The board itself will give you a list of such institutions. Alternatively, you may be able to sit the exam through an *open centre* run by the board. These are listed on page 27.

The deadline for entries varies from board to board. To be safe you should give details and confirmation of entry to the institution or body organising your exam by the end of January (for June exams) or the end of September (for exams taken in November and January).

Examining board entry confirmation

The board will confirm receipt of your exam entries. Check carefully that all the details are correct, in particular that you have been entered for the correct syllabus: remember that there is often more than one syllabus in a subject.

What you are allowed to take into the exam

In the case of many subjects and syllabuses you may be allowed to take aids with you into the exam. These may take the form of electronic calculators, dictionaries and prescribed texts that you have been studying. The examining board will make it clear in advance what you may and what you may not take into the exam. Check these regulations carefully well before the date of the exam itself.

Dyslexia

If you are dyslexic you may be entitled to special considerations. These may take the form of extra time in which to read the exam paper or write your answers. Alternatively, the examiners may give you sympathetic consideration when they convert the marks you have been given into a grade.

In order to obtain these considerations you must first visit an educational psychologist and ask that your learning skills be assessed and described in a report. Send this report to the examining board via the institution organising your exam.

This report must follow a consultation that has taken place within the 12 months preceding the date of the exam you are sitting. Whether or not you are then given any concessions is entirely at the discretion of the board.

Results

The results of your A-level exams will not be sent by the examining board to you directly but to the school or college where you sat the exam, from where they will be passed on to you.

In the case of A-levels sat in June the results will arrive on the Thursday following the third Wednesday in August. The results for January modules are published in March.

Appeals

If you feel your result is wrong it is possible to request that the examiners review your scripts. Such 're-marks', for which the board makes a charge (refunded if you are eventually upgraded) take several forms. You may simply ask for a clerical check in order to ascertain that the marks you were given were added up properly. Alternatively you may ask that your scripts are reread by a senior examiner and reassessed. You may also, if you wish, ask for a report on your script – something that may help you to understand where you went wrong.

Bear in mind that very few requests for the re-marking of scripts result in an improved grade.

Certificates

Some time after the results of an A-level examination session are published you will receive a certificate, confirming the grade you obtained for each subject.

A-level specifications

SUBJECT CRITERIA

As mentioned in the overview on page 2, most A-level subjects reflect the *subject criteria* laid down by the QCA. These are available on the web at www.qca.org.uk.

Subject criteria are intended to:

- help ensure consistent and comparable standards in the same subject across the awarding bodies

- define the relationship between AS and A-level specifications

- ensure that the standard of A-level is maintained

- help universities and employers know what has been studied and assessed.

The subject criteria contain the following sections:

1 Aims

- The skills and understanding the specification should encourage students to develop eg skills of analysis, interpretation and evaluation.

- What the specification should enable the students to achieve within the subject, eg enable the study of cognitive, social and physiological psychology.

2 Specification content

This gives notice of any prior requirements expected before commencement of study, eg for A-level Design & Technology the specification is expected to build on knowledge already gained at National Curriculum Key Stage 4. Many subject criteria express no such expectation however.

This section details the knowledge, understanding and skills that it is expected will be developed during the course of study. A summary of this part of the criteria is included with the individual subject section in the second half of this book.

3 Key skills

There are six key skills that are acknowledged to be of primary importance to both employers and universities alike, no matter what subjects you are studying. These are:

- communication

- information technology

- application of number

- improving own learning and performance

- working with others

- problem solving.

The first three are sometimes called the *hard* key skills (because they are easier to test rather than being any more difficult), and these form the basis of the *Key Skills Qualification*, see page 38 for more information. Both A-level and GNVQ specifications identify opportunities for developing and generating evidence for key skills assessment. Often such opportunities are directly cross-referenced to the elements of the specifications for the Key Skills Qualification. Such cross-referencing is called *signposting*. The subject criteria set out which key skills are expected in terms of opportunities for development. For example Application of Number is the only key skill not required of specifications in History, whilst opportunities to develop all six need to be present in Psychology.

4 Assessment objectives

The assessment objectives give details of the skills to be assessed and their relative weightings in both AS and A-level specifications. For example in Psychology knowledge and understanding of psychological theories are weighted as 45–55% of AS specifications, but only 40–50% of the full A-level.

5 Scheme of assessment

The subject criteria lay down the maximum percentage of the total marks a specification can allocate to internal assessment such as coursework or projects that are marked by the teacher and then moderated by the awarding body. This differs from subject to subject: in Music the maximum percentage for the internally assessed component is 50% whereas in History only 30% is allowed.

A minimum of 20% of marks for all A-level specifications should be devoted to *synoptic* assessment. Synoptic assessment seeks to cover the entire qualification rather than being specific to the subject matter of a particular module. The subject criteria give examples of synoptic assessment tasks. The following is such an example for Psychology:

A piece of written work in which the candidates draw on a range of theoretical approaches to consider a contemporary debate in Psychology, for example the controversies surrounding behavioural genetics.

6 Grade descriptions

These indicate the level of attainment characteristic of a given grade at A-level in terms of the required learning outcomes. Descriptions relating to grades A, C and E are offered within the criteria for each subject.

A-level specifications

LINEAR & MODULAR MODES OF STUDY

A-levels are normally offered as six modules or units. AS-levels comprise three modules that are a subset of the full A-level and are normally studied as year 1 of the full A-level course. Modules provide opportunities for synoptic assessment (see the section on subject criteria) and many also include those relating to coursework that is assessed by the teacher. In some specifications optional modules are available, although in reality this is often an option for the teacher delivering the specification rather than for the student receiving it. Examples of options are included in the subject details in the second half of this book.

Students may take unit assessments throughout the course, which is termed *modular assessment*, or at the end of the course, which is termed *linear assessment*. Examination sessions are available in January and June, although all modules may not be available for examination at all times during the two-year life of a specification. Different institutions, departments and teachers will also take a view on the order of teaching, timing of assessment and combination of modules and this may influence student choice as to where to embark on an A-level course.

For example a decision may be made that no examinations will be taken in January of year 1 as students may be unable to cope with the higher level of study (compared with that of GCSE) at this early stage. All three AS modules are taken in a linear fashion in the June of year 1 to allow students the opportunity to enter year 2 with a bankable qualification. In year 2 a single module is taken in January to spread the burden of assessment and the final two modules taken in June of that year.

Relative advantages and disadvantages of linear and modular assessment are given below.

In linear or terminally assessed specifications you spend two years learning a subject and at the end of that time a few hours being examined on it. The modular approach, on the other hand, divides the subject matter into separate 'chunks' or modules of learning, and assesses and grades you after you have been taught the content of each module. The marks obtained on each module are later added together and turned into a final A-level grade.

There are a number of advantages to the modular approach. Perhaps the most important is that it keeps you on your toes throughout the whole of your programme of study. The regularity of modular assessments provides a series of short-term goals, helping you to maintain your motivation.

The modular approach also provides you with regular feedback on your performance and enables you to monitor and, if necessary, improve your final grade. If you have fallen below par in an early module you can work out how much better you are going to have to do on the remaining ones in order to reach the standard you require – or alternatively you may decide to retake the early module before including its mark in your final grade.

There are some disadvantages. Much A-level subject matter does not fit easily into six neat module-sized slots. Subjects like Economics, Mathematics and Chemistry depend on a core theory that cannot easily be broken up: learning one bit of the specification depends on understanding another. If you split a subject up into self-contained units you fragment the continuity required to grasp the backbone of the subject. 'Integrated' learning and understanding of the theoretical core of a subject is downgraded in favour of 'applied' learning. This, some teachers argue, is to put the cart before the horse.

However, the most important point to grasp about the modular approach to A-levels is that it requires different skills from those demanded by the traditional exams. These favour students who possess (among other qualities) what are essentially good journalistic skills – the ability to synthesise two years' worth of facts and understanding into a few short essays, composed against the relentless deadline of the clock. No amount of knowledge or understanding counts for very much unless you possess this skill. Modular A-levels, with their reliance on coursework and frequent assessments, favour students who don't like to be rushed and who dislike cramming two-years' work for one set of exams. Traditional A-levels favour students with good memories who have learned how to present a small number of carefully selected facts relevantly and lucidly.

Validity of modules

The 'shelf-life' of modules will be as long as that specification remains current. Students who wish to delay certification should check with the awarding body as to any intentions to make major revisions to the specification(s) involved.

Cashing modules & certification

Unlike previous modular A-level schemes, candidates are no longer able to refuse certification in order to resit in an attempt to achieve a higher grade. Modules are 'banked' until such time as they qualify for certification.

Retaking modular syllabuses

Only one resit per module is available. If a specification demands that modules should be taken in a set order then any resits must occur in timing with the rest of the course; eg a student would not be able to resit an AS unit required for A2 study in the June of the second year of the course.

AS-levels

From September 2000 the AS-level will change both its name and its nature. The name will change from *Advanced Supplementary Level* to *Advanced Subsidiary Level*.

The new AS-level is designed to have 40% of the content of the full A-level with lower weighting on synoptic assessment (see page 13). The qualification attracts half the UCAS points for university entry as does the full A-level, and could therefore be seen as an easy option. It is unlikely however, that many candidates will apply to higher education with six AS-levels rather than the traditional three A-levels.

The content of AS-levels forms the first part of the full A-level specification and is designed to be studied as the first year of a two-year A-level course. This has the potential advantage that students who fail to return for their second year of study, for whatever reason, are able to leave with a qualification of value. AS-levels do not need to be studied as the first year of a full A-level, however. The government introduced the qualification in the hope and expectation that students would broaden their areas of study by taking more AS subjects in the first year of their two-year A-level course. Thus a student might study four or five AS-levels in year 1 but only take three of them to the full A-level in year 2. AS-levels do not have to be completed in one year and some institutions, particularly colleges of further education, offer *thin* AS-level courses where the content is spread over two years and is taken alongside the main course of study, which may be a BTEC National Diploma in Animal Care or Diploma in Nursery Nursing.

The AS-level specification comprises three modules of study and as previously discussed these are available for examination in January and June. The qualification has a vocational equivalent in the Vocational A-level three unit award.

Advanced Extension Awards

Advanced Extension Awards (or AEAs) replace the *Special* or *S-level* papers for the year 2002 onwards. Initially they are available in five subjects: Chemistry, English, French, Geography and Mathematics. Subject availability is set to increase on completion of the pilot phase. AEAs are targeted at the top 10% of students in each subject and designed to meet the following objectives.

AEAs should:

- stretch the most able A-level students and help differentiate candidates for university entrance

- ensure that UK students are tested against standards comparable with the most demanding in other countries (AEAs are sometimes known as *World Class Tests*)

- be accessible to all students regardless of which awarding body A-level specification they are studying.

AEAs are based on the A-level subject criteria (see page 11). They require a greater depth of understanding of a particular subject rather than a greater breadth of knowledge and require application of understanding in critical analysis, evaluation and synthesis within the subject. AEAs should not require any teaching additional to that appropriate to A-level study.

AEAs are graded as *Distinction, Merit* or *Unclassified*. Whilst they are highly valued by university admissions tutors, they are not allocated a points score by UCAS (see page 20).

A-level grades

A-level papers, modules and other performances are given marks that are then turned into grades. There are six possible grades that may be finally awarded – five pass grades and one fail grade. The pass grades are A, B, C, D, E. The fail grade is U or unclassified.

In some subjects an individual component in the exam, such as an oral assessment, is given its own grade and this will appear on your results slip as a suffix to the grade for the exam as a whole.

Your whole A-level performance – taking account of all the subjects examined – may be measured by converting each A-level and AS-level grade into points. The number of points attached to each grade is shown in the box below. It can be seen that if you obtain two A-level passes with a B and a C grade and two AS-level passes, both at D grades, you will score 240 points.

Vocational A-levels and key skills units at levels 2 and 3 are also allocated UCAS points, as are Scottish qualifications. The table below shows the point score or *Tariff* for different grades of the various qualifications.

UCAS TARIFF

Single units		GCE A/AS and Vocational A-level			Score	Scottish Framework Qualifications			
Main key skills[1]	1-unit award[2]	3-unit award	6-unit award	12-unit award	**Score**	Advanced Higher[3]	Higher	Inter-mediate 2	Standard grade credit
				A	**240**				
				B	**200**				
				C	**160**				
			A	D	**120**	A			
			B		**100**	B			
			C	E	**80**	C			
					72		A		
		A	D		**60**		B		
		B			**50**				
					48		C		
					42			A	
		C	E		**40**				
					38				Band 1
					35			B	
Level 4		D			**30**				
					28			C	Band 2
Level 3	A	E			**20**				
	B				**17**				
	C				**13**				
Level 2	D				**10**				
	E				**7**				

[1] Aggregate individual unit scores for Key Skills Qualification. [2] Covers stand-alone GCE Advanced Mathematics units, and Vocational A-level units over and above those required to achieve the 12-unit award. [3] Subsumes achievement of Higher in same subject.

Where A-levels may be studied

A number of different types of education providers offer A-level study.

Comprehensive school

Unless they have 'opted out', comprehensive schools are run by LEAs and form the backbone of secondary education in this country. Some local authorities link the sixth forms of several comprehensive schools under their control in order to widen the facilities available to all sixth-formers in their area.

Sixth-form college

In some parts of the country sixth-form education is no longer the responsibility of the local education authority. Instead, self-governing sixth-form colleges, funded by the Further Education Funding Council, fulfil the function of the school sixth form, enabling those who wish to remain in education after their GCSEs to study A-levels.

Further Education college

These cater for students aged 16 and over as well as adults. In addition to A-levels they are likely to offer a range of other courses. FE colleges often provide the best opportunity for someone who has left school to obtain A-levels. Many offer a wide range of well-taught courses and provide a pleasant and relaxed environment in which to learn. You may be asked to pay towards the cost of your course (depending on your circumstances) but the sums involved are not likely to be large. Colleges of this type are financed by the Further Education Funding Council.

Independent school

There are over 500 independent schools in this country (confusingly known as 'public schools') – some of which are ancient foundations with reputations for social exclusivity and (generally) academic excellence. They may be boarding or day schools, co-educational or single-sex. Staff-student ratios are usually, but not always, better than in local authority schools, but fees are high. Good independent schools are selective in their admissions and entry may be quite competitive; but in the last few years many well-known independent schools have seen applications drop and admission has become easier. Information about independent schools may be obtained from ISIS (see details below).

Independent sixth-form college

There are a number of independent sixth-form colleges that offer excellent opportunities to undertake A-level study. These colleges, that usually admit students on both a boarding and a day basis, cater for those who leave school at the age of 16 as well as for the slightly older student. They also offer one of the most effective ways to retake an A-level.

The best of these colleges are characterised by excellent staff-student ratios, close attention to individual needs and a wide choice of subjects. However, they charge high fees and must be chosen with care. As a general rule, it is a good idea to attend only a college that has been accredited by the Independent Schools Joint Council or recognised as efficient by the British Accreditation Council (BAC), or one that has been recommended to you on the basis of personal experience. Further information about independent sixth-form colleges may be obtained from independent educational consultants such as Gabbitas (see details below).

Adult evening classes

Most local authorities run a wide selection of evening classes that are open to any suitably motivated student (adult or younger) who wishes to pursue a hobby or an interest or to learn something new. Most of these classes develop practical or physical skills, from upholstery to aerobics; but a few are designed for those who wish to learn an academic subject, sometimes with the aim of taking an A-level at the end of it. Your local authority will publish a list of the classes it runs, including any suitable for A-level candidates.

Distance learning

What used to be known as a correspondence course can be an effective way of studying. It is not, however, a suitable way of preparing for an A-level unless you are highly motivated and organised and do not need – as even the best students usually do – the regular stimulus and approval of a teacher. It can also be a very lonely way of studying. Further information about distance learning may be obtained from Gabbitas (see box, below).

Private tutor

A private tutor can sometimes be the best compromise between a full-time course in a college and a correspondence course. The particular advantage of learning in this way is that you remain in control over how much tuition you receive. The difficulty is finding a tutor who is both experienced and dedicated enough to help you do justice in the A-level exam. If you want to find a private tutor, approach any good local school or college with a sixth form and ask whether they have a member of staff who would be prepared to take you on. Tuition is likely to take place in the evening or at weekends. You will probably have to pay the tutor by the hour.

For further information about...

Comprehensive schools
Your local education authority

Sixth-form colleges
Public libraries

Tertiary colleges
Your local education authority

Independent schools
The ISIS Association
56 Buckingham Gate
London SW1L 6AG
Tel: 020 7630 8793

Independent sixth-form colleges
Gabbitas
6–8 Sackville Street
London W1X 2BR
Tel: 020 7734 0161

Adult evening classes
Your local education authority

Distance learning
Gabbitas (see above)

Private tutors
Any local school
Newspaper advertisements

How A-levels are examined

A-level assessment takes a wide variety of shapes and forms. Most subjects are assessed by the traditional *written exam* that is sat under strictly controlled, timed, conditions. Written exams are normally one and a half hours per module and consist of questions requiring different types of answers. Many call for free-ranging *essays*, which you may be allowed up to 45 minutes to write; others demand some shorter *data response* answers (in response to some information or a diagram given on the question paper). Some written papers simply require candidates to select one of four possible answers to around 40 questions in a type of paper known as a *multiple choice exam* or an *objective test*. Language A-levels, of course, usually require written translations.

It is increasingly common for part of the exam to consist of a piece of work done in your own time before the exam itself. This takes the form of a *project* or *extended essay* with a title that has been agreed with the examining board beforehand. In some cases this type of assessment forms a compulsory part of the exam; in others it is either an optional extra or an optional alternative (taken instead of part of the written exam). Projects and extended essays favour those who are not good at performing against the clock, but who are good at research and organising themselves so that the work is completed before the deadline for submission.

A similar form of assessment is known as *coursework*. This consists not of a single essay but of a series of essays written over the two-year period spent studying for the A-level. You will be quite familiar with this form of assessment since it is widely used for the GCSE, though its use is not nearly so widespread at A-level.

Some subjects lend themselves to being assessed by *oral exam*. This is most usual with modern languages, for which you must take part in a conversation in the language you are studying so that your spoken skills may be gauged. Other subjects are examined orally in different ways and for different reasons. In some cases visiting examiners come to talk to students about project work they have done.

Modern language exams also make use of what is known as an *aural exam* or *listening comprehension* in which you are required to listen to a tape-recording of the language you have studied and to answer questions that test how much you have understood.

The assessment of science and technical subjects (such as Biology, Chemistry, Physics, Geology, Art & Design, Photography) includes *practical exercises.* Most are now assessed internally but practical examinations are offered in some specifications. Art & Design students are sometimes given two to three weeks in which to complete practical assignments.

As an alternative to timed practical assessments, performances in some subjects are assessed by marking much of the practical work done throughout the two years as *coursework.* The assessment of other subjects (such as Design & Technology) requires you to engage in a *practical project*, approved by the board in advance and completed in your own time during the course of your studies.

Examining methods – a summary

Timed written exam

> Essays

> Data response questions

> Multiple choice/objective test

Project or extended essay

Coursework

Oral exam

Aural (listening) comprehension

Timed practical

Coursework practical

Practical project

Where A-levels are examined

It is normal for A-level candidates to sit their exams at the institution where they have been studying. Any educational establishment that prepares students for their A-levels will run the necessary exams at the end of the course. However, if you have studied through a correspondence course or just with the help of a private tutor, or even without any teaching at all, there may be no obvious place for you to sit the exam. What should you do then?

You may take one of two steps. If you are sitting an A-level set by the AQA you may approach one of its two 'open centres' (listed below) as a *private* candidate. However, open centres are not run by the other examining boards; furthermore, some syllabuses are not open to private candidates at open centres.

The alternative course of action is to contact the examining board that sets the syllabus you are following and ask for a list of the names and addresses of all the educational establishments in your area that run exams set by that board. You should then ring any of the schools or colleges on the list and ask whether they would be prepared to allow you to sit your A-levels with them as an *external candidate*. Whether they do or not is entirely at their discretion, and if they do they will be entitled to charge you an exam centre fee to cover their costs in addition to the exam entry fee that is payable to the board.

For several reasons you may find it absolutely impossible to find somewhere to sit your A-level exam. Some boards do not run open centres and you may not be able to find a local school or college willing to take you on as an external candidate when the time comes to sit your exam. Some subjects and syllabuses involve coursework that has to be assessed by a teacher, or may require other forms of assessment involving practical work (eg Biology, Chemistry, Physics) or spoken and listening exercises (eg modern languages). It can be difficult and sometimes impossible to be examined in these subjects unless the exam is organised where you have been studying the A-level.

It is, therefore, essential to check that you have somewhere to sit your A-level before embarking on a course of study.

AQA

Open centres for private candidates

The London Open Centre
The Associated Examining Board
Stag Hill House
Guildford, Surrey GU2 5XJ
Tel: 01483 506506

Liverpool Centre
Education & Lifelong Service
Awards Section
4th Floor
4 Renshaw Street
Liverpool L1 4NX
Tel: 0151 233 2855

Who marks A-levels?

For the most part A-levels are marked by external examiners appointed by the examining board whose syllabuses you are following. Work completed in a timed exam or during the term is sent by post to the examiner, who marks it and passes the result to the board. Different papers in the same exam will probably be marked by different examiners, depending upon their speciality.

Sometimes it is necessary for the external examiners to visit the school or college where you are studying or sitting the exam. This happens for many Modern Language oral exams (though some of these are now recorded and the tape sent to the examiner) and for the assessment of drama, music and physical artefacts which are too bulky to be sent by post.

A few forms of assessment are internal. These include the assessment of coursework, whether written or practical, and of some project work. In these cases the teacher in charge of the work or project awards what he or she judges to be the correct and fair mark according to guidelines issued by the board. The board then spot-checks some marks and 'moderates' all marks – that is to say, adjusts them up or down according to whether they think a particular school or teacher is being generally too severe or too lenient.

Once all parts of the syllabus have been assessed, the marks awarded for each part are added together to produce what is known as a 'raw mark'. The examining board's chief examiner and staff then convert the raw mark into a final grade. The correlation of raw marks to grade bands remains more or less constant from year to year though the precise boundaries vary slightly as the board tries to compensate for what it reckons may be unusually hard or easy papers in any one year.

A-level assessment is a difficult and complicated task. It requires experience and fine judgement as well as careful collating and adding up of all the marks. Amidst all the thousands of scripts marked each year it is inevitable that mistakes will occur and you can, if you wish, challenge a result. Such a challenge may take several forms. You may simply ask for a clerical check to be conducted on your scripts to see that the marks were added up correctly; or you may ask the examiners to re-read what you wrote and think again about the marks awarded in the first place. You may also go a stage further and ask that they write a report on your performance.

Very few A-levels are re-marked in this way and of those which are only a very small proportion result in an improved grade. Since the examining boards make a charge for these second assessments (refundable if your result is eventually upgraded) you should take careful advice from a teacher before requesting a re-mark.

A-level examiners

External examiners who:

Mark written work
Conduct oral exams
Assess practical work.

Internal examiners (usually your teacher) who:

Mark coursework
Mark projects.

Retaking A-levels

Modules may be retaken in the January and June sessions following the original, subject to the constraints described on page 16.

Coursework, orals & practicals

Many A-levels involve assessment of work or skills that do not form part of a written examination – such as coursework and oral/practical work. One of three procedures applies for those retaking such subjects:

- the *option* either to carry forward the mark from the first occasion without doing further work; or submit to a fresh assessment – in the case of coursework, after it has been reworked

- the *obligation* to carry forward the mark given on the first occasion without doing further work

- the *obligation* to submit to a second assessment – in the case of coursework, after it has been reworked.

How long will it take?

You will probably wish to resit an A-level syllabus or module as soon as possible after your first attempt and often this is the most sensible course of action. While motivation provided by a poor result is at its strongest, the effort put into a revision programme is likely to be at its greatest; moreover, memory fades quickly.

However, common sense must prevail, and you may need a year to raise your grade. The time needed will reflect several factors, including the reasons for your original poor performance, your motivation and ability, the degree of improvement you seek and your overall workload.

A year's course may be necessary:

- if your original result reflected work missed rather than just bad revision or poor exam technique

- if there are any grounds for doubting your ability to make the necessary improvement in just one term

- if more than two A-levels need to be retaken in the same term.

In all cases seek advice first.

University attitudes towards retaking

It is widely believed that universities are reluctant to accept applicants who have taken their A-levels more than once, but this is rarely the case. It is true that universities offering the more competitive degree courses (such as Business Studies) sometimes require slightly higher grades from those who have had to retake A-levels; but it is only a very few universities that refuse to consider such applicants at all.

Such difficulties should not form part of an argument against retaking exams: they can only serve as a warning to the pre-A-level candidate that things will not become easier. It is, however, essential that you check the attitude towards retakers of any university to which you wish to apply.

Chances of improvement

There are no guarantees that retaking will end in a better result. A disappointing first-time outcome may sometimes reflect intractable problems for which intensive revision and repeated exams are not the best answer. Nevertheless, most people do improve their performance on retaking – some by a considerable margin. There are good grounds for expecting an improvement:

- Chance plays its part: most exam papers cannot be assessed entirely objectively and variations in standards may make a second try worthwhile.

- You will probably be studying fewer subjects when retaking than on the first attempt. In most cases the syllabus will have been covered before, allowing time to concentrate on areas of weakness and exam technique.

- Numbers of students retaking are usually smaller, with a consequent improvement in teacher-student ratios.

- You will be older and more mature when retaking, and probably a more efficient learner.

- If your first performance failed to match your ability on account of laziness you may find in that failure sufficient motivation for a more successful second attempt.

- If your original failure can be attributed to an external cause such as illness, bad teaching or a poor teacher-student relationship, a retake course in changed circumstances will probably allow you a better chance of success.

- Finally, it must be said that schools are concerned with wider educational objectives, and the pure pursuit of exam success must often compete with other activities. A course of study leading to the retaking of exams will have narrower and more specific goals.

A-level publications

Specifications

All A-level examining boards publish specifications that describe, often in some considerable detail, what you will be expected to know when you are assessed. Whilst it is the responsibility of those who teach you to note and follow these specifications carefully, reading them yourself will help you grasp what it is you are attempting to do during your two years of A-level study.

The specifications also make plain the parts that are compulsory and those you may determine yourself from a list of options given. In many cases the teacher or student has considerable choice – not only of different papers within a syllabus but of different topics within a paper.

A-level students also have a choice to make at a different level. Reading the specifications will make you aware that you may also choose from several on the same subject, since individual syllabuses of the more popular subjects are set by every or nearly every examining board.

Past papers

In addition to reading the specifications, you should also look carefully at past exam papers. These give the best indication of what you will face in the exam at the end of your course; and they may be used for valuable exam practice nearer the final exams themselves.

Past papers are obtainable from the examining boards but your school or college should have a set.

Marking schemes

When preparing for an A-level exam it can be very useful to know how it will be marked. Marking schemes make it clear how marks are allocated to each type of question and precisely what the examiners will be looking for in awarding these marks.

Examiners' reports

After each exam session the examiners in each subject publish a report on the performance of all those sitting the A-level. These reports cover candidates' performance across the country as a whole, not just in one school or college (though these may be specially requested).

Examiners' reports are a good and useful guide to what examiners are looking for and so how to prepare effectively for an A-level exam. They are published by the separate boards, from whom they are available on request.

Index of subjects & syllabuses

A-LEVEL & AS-LEVEL COURSES STARTING IN SEPTEMBER 2000

Subject submission	Awarding body				
	AQA	Edexcel	OCR	CCEA	WJEC
Accounting	✔		✔		
Ancient History			✔		
Arabic		✔			
Archaeology	✔				
Art	✔	✔	✔	✔	✔
Bengali	✔				
Biological Science	✔	✔	✔	✔	✔
Business Studies	✔	✔	✔	✔	✔
Chemistry	✔	✔	✔	✔	✔
Chinese		✔			
Classical Civilisation	✔		✔		
Classical Greek	✔		✔		
Communication Studies	✔				
Computing	✔	✔	✔		✔
Critical Thinking (AS only)			✔		
Dance	✔				
Design & Technology	✔	✔	✔		✔
Drama & Theatre Studies	✔	✔			✔
Dutch			✔		
Economics	✔	✔	✔	✔	✔
Economics & Business Studies		✔	✔		
Electronics	✔		✔		✔
English Language	✔	✔	✔		✔
English Language & Literature	✔	✔	✔		✔

Subject submission	Awarding Body				
	AQA	**Edexcel**	**OCR**	**CCEA**	**WJEC**
English Literature	✔	✔	✔	✔	✔
Environmental Science	✔				
European Studies (AS only)	✔				
Film Studies					✔
French	✔	✔	✔	✔	✔
General Studies	✔	✔	✔		
Geography	✔	✔	✔	✔	✔
Geology			✔		✔
German	✔	✔	✔		✔
Government & Politics	✔	✔	✔	✔	
Gujarati		✔			
Hindi*					
History	✔	✔	✔	✔	✔
History of Art	✔				
Home Economics	✔		✔	✔	
Information Technology	✔	✔	✔		
Irish				✔	
Italian		✔			
Japanese		✔			
Latin	✔		✔		
Law	✔		✔		✔
Mathematics	✔	✔	✔	✔	✔
Media Studies	✔		✔		✔
Modern Greek		✔			
Modern Hebrew	✔				
Music	✔	✔	✔	✔	✔
Music Technology		✔			
Panjabi	✔				
Performance Studies			✔		
Persian			✔		
Philosophy	✔				
Physical Education	✔	✔	✔		✔
Physics	✔	✔	✔	✔	✔

* Final decisions are yet to be reached about which awarding body will provide a specification in this subject.

Subject submission	Awarding Body				
	AQA	**Edexcel**	**OCR**	**CCEA**	**WJEC**
Polish	✔				
Portuguese			✔		
Psychology	✔	✔	✔		
Religious Studies	✔	✔	✔	✔	✔
Russian		✔			
Science			✔		
Science for Public Understanding (AS only)	✔				
Social Policy		✔			
Social Science: Citizenship (AS only)	✔				
Sociology	✔†		✔		✔†
Spanish	✔	✔	✔		✔
Turkish			✔		
Urdu		✔			
Welsh					✔
Welsh second language					✔
World Development (AS only)					✔

† Sociology: joint AQA and WJEC.

Key skills

The Key Skills Qualification

Most students aged 16–18 in full-time education will study key skills
as part of their A-level programme or its alternative. Key skills are
those skills identified by employers and universities as being vital to
the success of an individual no matter what their job or course of
study. There are six identified key skills:

- application of number

- communication

- information technology

- working with others

- problem solving

- improving own learning and performance.

The first three on the list are known as the *hard* key skills and form
the components of the *Key Skills Qualification*.

Application of number

As its name suggests, this skill deals with the use of Maths rather
than being a Maths course in its own right. It deals with abilities to
analyse data and to present your own data in such a way that it is
readily understood by others.

Communication

This skill deals with the way you present ideas in a group discussion,
presentation and in written communication.

Information technology

This skill covers the use of IT in communication and in data analysis and presentation. Skills in word processing, use of spreadsheets and databases are included here.

Each key skill is available for assessment at levels 1–5, which correspond to the levels of the National Qualification Framework (see page 41). The qualification is said to be *profiled* in that the three component key skills can be achieved at different levels. Very able students may take all three key skills at level 3 or even level 4 during their A-level course, but many will achieve one or more at level 2. Students on arts-based courses, for example, may find level 3, Application of Number, difficult to achieve.

Each key skill is assessed internally through the production of a *portfolio of evidence* in the same way as Vocational A-levels are assessed, and also via an external examination. The external tests at levels 1 and 2 are multi-choice questions whilst those for levels 3 upwards require extended written answers. Prior achievement of GCSE Maths or English at grades A*–C will allow students to be credited with the external component of Application of Number or Communication up to level 2. In other words, if you have these GCSEs you will not have to sit the exam, but you will still need to produce a portfolio of evidence.

Key skills elements at levels 2, 3 and 4 attract UCAS points (see page 20) and so contribute to the chances of gaining a place at university.

Section 2

Alternatives to A-levels

The National Qualification Framework (NQF)

At the heart of the work of the Qualifications and Curriculum Authority (QCA) is the establishment of a coherent national framework of qualifications, embracing three families of qualification – general (academic), general vocational and vocational, all underpinned by key skills. Qualifications will be approved into this framework at different levels:

- entry

- foundation

- intermediate

- advanced.

A-levels for example occupy a place AS-level 3 Advanced General qualifications.

The purpose of the qualifications that make up the national framework are often very different: NVQs, for example, are work-based qualifications that recognise what a person can do; GNVQs are school- or college-based qualifications that develop knowledge and skills in a vocational area. Comparisons should be considered, therefore, in the light of the different structures and purposes of the qualifications that make up the framework (see table on next page).

NATIONAL QUALIFICATION FRAMEWORK

Quals/levels	Entry	Level 1 Foundation	Level 2 Intermediate	Level 3 Advanced	Level 4	Level 5
Vocational	Common	eg Level 1 NVQ	eg Level 2 NVQ	eg Level 3 NVQ	eg Level 4 NVQ	eg Level 5 NVQ
General Vocational	to all	eg GNVQ Foundation	eg GNVQ Intermediate	eg GNVQ Advanced		
General (Academic)	families	eg GCSE (grades D–G)	eg GCSE (grades A–C)	eg GCE A/AS-level		

Key Skills

The alternatives

Courses of study leading to A-level exams are taken by half the 16-year-olds continuing their education in England, Wales and Northern Ireland. The remainder pursue one of the many alternatives to the A-level system and it is worth knowing what they are. They may suit you better.

These alternatives fall into two categories: *academic* programmes and *vocational* programmes.

Academic alternatives

There are two principal academic alternatives to A-levels: the Scottish Certificate of Education and the International Baccalaureate.

The Scottish Certificate of Education (which many Scottish schools pursue alongside A-levels) provides a more widely based programme in which you study up to six subjects.

The International Baccalaureate, as its name suggests, is an international exam system available in this country and many others. Its essential features are its breadth of subject and its 'portability': it may be studied almost anywhere in the world and is recognised by the universities of over 60 countries. It is described on pages 49–52.

Vocational alternatives

A-levels, Scottish Highers and the International Baccalaureate are essentially *academic* programmes. They are designed to increase knowledge and to develop intellectual skills. They will not train you for jobs, trades or professions or develop practical skills – which is what many 16-year-olds require of their education. All professions and industries are dependent on a steady inflow of young people who have learned trades or skills with which to earn their living; and if you wish to pursue such a path you will need to undergo appropriate technical training. This can take many forms, from a certificate in catering, beauty therapy or fashion to a diploma in accountancy, horticulture or engineering.

Vocational training is largely the responsibility of the three unitary awarding bodies: AQA, Edexcel and OCR. These bodies were formed between two or more 'academic' and 'vocational' partners. Thus AQA incorporates City & Guilds qualifications, Edexcel includes BTEC qualifications and OCR includes RSA qualifications. Amongst other qualifications all three offer the General National Vocational Qualification or GNVQ (see page 56) and also National Vocational Qualifications or NVQs. There are a large number of smaller, vocationally specific awarding bodies offering specialist qualifications, eg CACHE (Council for Awards in Children's Care and Education), which offers the very popular Diploma in Nursery Nursing (DNN).

All these alternatives to A-levels, academic and vocational, address drawbacks of the A-level system, which is sometimes criticised for being too limited in its aims and for concentrating on too narrow a range of skills in too few subject areas. For instance, the A-level system allows some students to emerge from full-time education at the age of 18 without in the previous two years having done any mathematics or written an essay; it allows others to concentrate on three science subjects at the expense of all other disciplines and forms of learning; it does not require any compulsory technical training. It is, in the view of some, too specialist and lopsided a form of education. Both the Scottish Certificate and the International Baccalaureate provide a more balanced approach to academic learning, whilst GNVQs and other qualifications awarded by the OCR, Edexcel and AQA offer a vocational alternative.

Sixth-form options – a summary

Academic options

Advanced levels (GCE examining boards)

Scottish Certificate of Education (Scottish Examination Board)

International Baccalaureate (Int. Baccalaureate Organisation)

Vocational programmes

GNVQs (City & Guilds, RSA, BTEC)

National Curriculum Certificates (City & Guilds)

Certificates (City & Guilds)

National Certificates (BTEC)

National Diplomas (BTEC)

The Scottish system

National Qualifications

Secondary education in Scotland follows a pattern which is significantly different from education in England, Wales and Northern Ireland, and 2000 saw the implementation of a revised qualifications system. The revised qualifications are called National Qualifications and are the counterpart of GCSEs and A-levels.

Under the government development programme known as Higher Still, the post-16 qualifications framework was developed to replace the SCE Higher. Under the banner of National Qualifications there are five levels: Access; Intermediate 1; Intermediate 2; Higher; and Advanced Higher. Higher courses have the same value as the original Scottish Certificate of Education (SCE) Higher, and four or five passes at Higher will still be the most common entry requirement for higher education.

The objective of the reform was to provide better progression between Standard Grade and Higher and to provide a greater breadth of study. There are 70 subjects in the framework, some are job orientated such as Travel and Tourism, and others are along more traditional lines such as History, Maths and English. It is not expected that schools will offer the full portfolio of subjects, some of which are more suited to college provision.

Standard Grades, which have not changed their format, have been brought under the National Qualifications heading.

The Building Blocks

The new National Qualifications framework is built up of units, courses and group awards. With the exception of Standard Grade courses, theses are all offered at five levels:

- National Units – The smallest element is called a unit and the majority require 40 hours of study. Units are internally assessed

- Courses

  Standard Grades are usually done in S4, at one of three levels: foundation, general and credit. Awards are made in terms of a seven point scale 1–7, where 1 is the highest award. Most Standard Grades are assessed on the basis of examination and an internally assessed element, such as a project or investigation.

  National Courses are usually taken in S5 or S6, and at college. They are made up of three units plus up to an additional 40 hours extra study. Each unit is internally assessed and in addition there is an exam which informs the grade awarded for the course – A, B, or D – with A being the highest award.

- Scottish group awards (SGAs) – SGAs are coherent programmes of courses and units which cover a particular subject area. There are 16 broad areas of study, such as Art and Design, Computing and Information Technology, or Land and Environment. An SGA can be attained within one year, or worked towards over a longer period of study. Previous achievements, such as Standard Grades, can also be credited towards an SGA.

Core skills

Similar to key skills in England and Wales, these are the skills we need to do well in education and training, to succeed in work, and to get on in life:

- Problem solving
- Communication
- Numeracy
- Information technology
- Working with others.

All National Qualifications have core skills embedded in them, but it is also possible to take stand-alone units.

Phasing arrangements

SCE Higher Grades were available for the last time in 2000. Certificate of Sixth Year Studies will be offered for the last time in

2001. For qualifications which have been wholly replaced through Higher Still – General Scottish Vocational Qualifications (GSVQs), Lifestart, Workstart, some National Certificate Clusters, National Certificate Modules and Short Courses – the last certification will be in the year 2004.

Certification

The Scottish Qualification Certificate is a cumulative record of all the qualifications a candidate has achieved to date, including a core skills profile.

Scottish Qualifications Authority

The Scottish Qualifications Authority (SQA) develops and awards most of the qualifications including National Qualifications, on offer in Scotland's schools, colleges, workplaces and education centres.

For more information about:

- SQA qualifications: call the SQA Helpdesk on 0141 242 2214

- Subject choices at school: talk to your Guidance Teacher or Careers Advisor

- Career information:

  - call Learning Direct Scotland on 0800 100 900

  - visit their website on: http://www.learning-direct-scotland.org.uk

Scottish Qualifications Authority

Hanover House   Ironmills Road
24 Douglas Street   Dalkeith
Glasgow   Midlothian
G2 7NQ   EH22 1LE

Helpdesk: 0141 242 2214   Website: http://www.sqa.org.uk
email: mail@sqa.org.uk

International Baccalaureate

The International Baccalaureate (IB) is a two-year sixth-form programme of study for young people aged between 16 and 19 who may wish to proceed afterwards to university in this country or others.

Since it is followed in more than 70 countries, the IB serves to provide schools all over the world with a common curriculum and matriculation examination which has wide acceptability. Further, it enables a growing internationally mobile community to find a secondary education overseas which will enable them to attend a university in their own country. One of the essential features of the IB is its requirement that you pursue your studies in more than one language. There are three working languages: English, French and Spanish.

The significant difference between the IB and its A-level counterpart is the more structured form of the IB: six subjects have to be studied alongside a course in the Theory of Knowledge, and there is a requirement that you undertake a series of activities representing Creativity, Action & Service, known as CAS. Moreover, the choice of subject combination is limited and tightly controlled (see page 51) and everything is examined together: subjects may not be taken piecemeal as they may at A-level.

Despite these differences, the IB is assessed in a way that is similar to A-levels. A written exam at the end of the course is supplemented by an extended essay in one of the chosen subjects.

Grades and awards

Students working for the IB must:

- accumulate at least 24 points: points are awarded to each IB subject examined, according to the scale:

1 *very poor*	5 *good*
2 *poor*	6 *very good*
3 *mediocre*	7 *excellent*
4 *satisfactory*	

- complete satisfactorily

  - the Theory of Knowledge Course

  - the extended essay

  - CAS activities

Participating schools

The IB is offered by over 500 schools in more than 70 countries worldwide. Originally these tended to be independent schools, but some national education ministries are now experimenting with the system in state scools – as a complement to their national systems.

Examinations

- Written exams

  In the curriculum subjects at the end of the two-year period of study

- Extended essay

  In one of the IB subjects

Progression

The IB is recognised as meeting the entrance requirements of the universities and other institutions of higher education in more than 60 countries, including the UK, most European Union countries and the US. IB students have entered more than 700 universities worldwide.

International Baccalaureate curriculum

Six subjects

At least three subjects (no more than four) must be at *Higher Level* and the remainder at *Subsidiary Level* from the following list, with no more than one subject from each group:

Group 1 – First Language

Language A1 (mother tongue); with study of some world literature

Group 2 – Second Language

Language A2 (strong ability) *or* language B (good ability) *or Ab initio* language (from scratch)

Group 3 – Individuals & Societies

Business & Organisation, History, Geography, Economics, Philosophy, Psychology, Social Anthropology

Group 4 – Experimental Sciences

Biology, Chemistry, General Chemistry, Applied Chemistry, Physics, Environmental Systems

Group 5 – Mathematics

Mathematics, Advanced Mathematics, Mathematical Methods, Mathematical Studies

Group 6 – General Subjects

Art/Design, Music, Latin, Greek, Computer Studies
or a school-based syllabus approved by the IBO
or a third modern language
or another subject from Group 3 or 4
or Advanced Mathematics

Theory of Knowledge course

Activities representing Creativity, Action & Service (CAS)

Further information

Head Office: International Baccalaureate Organisation (IBO)
Route des Morillons 15
CH-1218 Grand-Saconnex
Geneve, Switzerland
Tel: 0041 22 7910274

UK Office: International Baccalaureate Organisation (IBO)
Pascal Close
St. Mellons, Cardiff
South Glamorgan
Wales CF3 0YP
Tel: 02920 774000

BTEC

BTEC stands for Business & Technology Education Council and is a brand name for a number of qualifications offered by the Edexcel Foundation.

BTEC creates and assesses programmes in a very wide range of work-related areas, providing education and training, developing the ability to 'think and do', and awarding national qualifications to those who successfully complete its courses. There are part-time as well as full-time versions of nearly all the courses offered.

Qualifications of interest here are BTEC First and National Certificates/Diplomas. The BTEC National Diploma is a two A-level equivalent qualification as is the Vocational A-level 12 unit award.

BTEC First Certificates and Diplomas provide qualifications equivalent to the GCSE. For a student aged between 16 and 18 or in the sixth form, BTEC runs what are known as National Certificates (part time) and Diplomas (full time).

Entry requirements for the 16-year-old usually consist of four good GCSE passes or an NVQ level 2 or an intermediate GNVQ. Both the part-time Certificate and the full-time Diploma usually take two years.

BTEC national qualifications can lead to employment in relevant fields of work or may be used as a means of entry to higher levels of vocational or academic study – such as BTEC Higher National Certificates and Diplomas and degree courses.

Examples from the extensive range of subjects that may be studied are outlined below.

National Diplomas

Beauty Therapy

Built Environment

Builders' Merchants
Studies

Building Services

Engineering

Cartography

Civil Engineering
Studies

Construction

Construction & Land
Use

Environmental Health
Studies

Land Administration
Surveying

**Business & Finance and
Public Administration**

Business & Finance

Housing Studies

Public Administration

Caring

Caring Services

**Computing & Information
Systems**

Computer Studies

IT Applications

Design

Design: many
disciplines

Foundation Studies in
Art & Design

General Art & Design

Practical Archaeology

Printing

Restoration Studies

Distribution Studies

Engineering

Coal Mining

Coal Mining
Electrical Engineering

Coal Mining Mechanical
Engineering

Mine Surveying

Mining Engineering

Engineering: various
kinds

Horticulture

Hotel & Catering

Hotel, Catering &
Institutional Operations

Land & Countryside

Agricultural Merchanting

Agriculture: various
forms

Arboriculture

Fishery Studies

Floristry

Forestry

Horticulture: various forms

Landscape Studies

Rural Studies

Leisure & Media

European Leisure Studies

Leisure Studies

Media

Travel & Tourism

Nautical Studies

Maritime Technology

Materials Technology

Metals Technology

Nautical Science

Shipping & Transport

Studies

Performing Arts

Music Technology

Performing Arts

Stage: Design & Construction

Stage Management

Public Administration

Public Services

Science

Footwear

Furniture

Science: several disciplines

Textiles

GNVQs

General National Vocational Qualifications – known as GNVQs – are a vocational and practical alternative to the A-level system. They are designed to develop skills with which students can earn their living, to provide training, or preparation for training, rather than the more academic skills with which A-levels are concerned. They are, however, a quite acceptable method of entry into higher education.

The number of subjects in which a GNVQ may be studied is fairly limited. At present 14 subjects are available and these are listed in the box, below.

GNVQs are offered by all three unitary awarding bodies: Edexcel, AQA and OCR. The majority of GNVQ students follow Edexcel specifications and the contents of these are described in the second part of this book.

Types of GNVQ

There are three levels of GNVQ: Foundation at NQF Level 1, Intermediate at NQF Level 2 and Advanced at NQF Level 3. If you consult the diagram showing the National Qualification Framework on page 42 you will see that it is the Advanced GNVQ which is equivalent to A-levels.

Advanced GNVQs were renamed Vocational A-levels in 2000 and are available in three sizes of qualification:

- The Full Award with 12 units of assessment equivalent to two A-levels.

- The Single Award with six units of assessment equivalent to one A-level.

- The Part Award with three units of assessment equivalent to one AS-level.

GNVQ subjects

Art & Design	Engineering
Business	Information & Communication Technology
Health & Social Care	
Leisure & Recreation	Media: Communication & Production
Manufacturing	
Construction & Built Environment	Performing Arts
Hospitality & Catering	Retail & Distributive Services
Science	Travel & Tourism

All subjects are available as Full and Single Awards but only four subjects are currently available as Part Awards. These are Business, Health & Social Care, Information & Communication Technology, and Engineering.

The three awards are subsets of each other in that the Part Award forms three units of the Single Award and the Single Award forms six units of the Full Award. The Single Awards as A-level equivalents are described in the second part of the book.

Entry Requirements

There are no set entry requirements for GNVQs. Entry to Vocational A-level GNVQ Full Award is likely to be an appropriate achievement at GNVQ Intermediate level, BTEC First Diploma or four GCSEs at grades C or above. It is likely that the six-unit Vocational A-levels will be studied in a mixed programme with GCE A-levels, where the institute's admission norms for any A-level programme are likely to apply.

Assessment and grades

Students who take the Full Award study six compulsory units and six from a variety of optional units. As with A-levels the options may be chosen by the teacher rather than being available to the student. Three of the compulsory units will be externally examined together with one from the optional units. GNVQs have a minimum of 33% external assessment. Internal assessment of GNVQs is through the building of a *Portfolio of Evidence*, often based largely on a number of assignments or small projects. Students who take six-unit Vocational A-levels study two externally assessed compulsory units, two internally assessed compulsory units and two internally assessed units from a variety of options.

Vocational A-levels are graded A–E, as are GCE A-levels. The six-unit Vocational A-level attracts the same number of UCAS points as its academic equivalent. The Full Award attracts double the UCAS points in line with its two A-level equivalence.

Vocational A-level (6 Unit Award)

ART & DESIGN

Compulsory Units (Block A)

2D Visual Language	portfolio assessment	Carry out exploratory work and develop two-dimensional visual language skills in different art, craft and design contexts.
3D Visual Language	portfolio assessment	Through exploratory work carry out investigations about formal elements, materials and technology, how to use 3D visual language for communication and analysis.

Optional Units (Block B)

One of the following:

Historical & Contextual Referencing	portfolio assessment	Become familiar with a wide range of historical and contemporary work by artists, craftspeople and designers.
Visual Communication & Meaning	external assessment	How visual language communicates meanings, messages and information in your own and others' work. How to use signs, symbols and images.

Optional Units (Block C)

Three from a choice of 25, one of which must be externally assessed. Externally assessed units in this block are *Working to Set Briefs* and *Create and Develop Ideas*. There are 23 units assessed by portfolio including *Fine Art Materials, Techniques and Technology, Sculpture, Narrative Image Making, Fashion Visualisation, Multimedia Technology, Moving Images* and *Exploring Ceramic Techniques*.

Moving on

Combined with other A-levels, the Vocational A-Level in Art & Design can lead to courses and careers in:

• Multimedia Design

• Architecture

• Advertising

• Marketing

• Film & Television

• Theatre or Costume Design.

BUSINESS

Compulsory Units (Block A)

Business at Work	portfolio assessed	Different types of business organisations and their functions and structures. How and why business objectives are set. Business communications and the impact of quality requirements on production and the business as a whole.
The Competitive Business Environment	externally assessed	Operation in the competitive market and the importance of competitiveness for survival. The effects of supply and demand, competition, government policy and the need for international competitiveness.

Marketing	portfolio assessed	The importance of business meeting the needs of the customer whilst ensuring profitability. Recognition of customer needs and the development of strategies to meet them.
Human Resources	portfolio assessed	People as a key resource of businesses. The importance of human resource planning for effective utilisation and management. Recruitment and selection, training and development and performance management.
Business Finance	externally assessed	Control and monitoring of finances. Construction and interpretation of financial statements. Budgeting and cash flow management.

Optional Units (Block B)

One unit from a choice of 18, four of which are externally assessed. Titles include: *Business Planning, Market Research, Business Statistics, ICT in Business; International Trade* and *Business Law.*

Moving on

Combined with other A-levels, a Vocational A-level in Business can lead to a university course or employment in the following areas:

- Accounting
- Marketing
- Personnel
- Retailing.

CONSTRUCTION & THE BUILT ENVIRONMENT

Compulsory Units (Block A)

The Built Environment & its Development	external assessment	Introduction to historical and present day development, construction and conservation of the built environment.
Design for Construction & the Built Environment	external assessment	Develop awareness of spatial organisation. Basic design and drawing techniques.
Town Planning & Development	portfolio assessment	Influence of town planning on area development.

Complete all in Block B or all in Block C.

Optional Units (Block B)

Science & Materials	portfolio assessment	Understanding of scientific principles and knowledge of the properties of materials.
Structures, Construction Technology & Services	portfolio assessment	Performance of buildings in terms of structural stability, safety and fitness for purpose.
Surveying Processes	portfolio assessment	Skills and knowledge of general building evaluation.

Optional Units (Block C)

Resource Management, Finance and the Built Environment and one other taken from a choice of 20 including *Civil Engineering Drawing, Environmental Science, Applied Mathematics, Housing Development* and *Planning and Development Controls.*

Moving on

Combined with other A-levels, the Vocational A-level in Construction & the Built Environment can lead to courses and careers in:

- Civil Engineering

- Architecture.

ENGINEERING

Compulsory Units (Block A)

Engineering Materials	external assessment	Structure, properties and behaviour of a range of materials. Links between properties and performance.
Design Development	External assessment	The design development cycle starting with a design brief. Production, selection and presentation of the most appropriate solution.

Optional Units (Block B)

Applied Science in Engineering	portfolio assessment	Understanding of the use of energy in products and systems. Application of scientific laws and principles that underpin both electrical and mechanical applications.
Applied Mathematics in Engineering	portfolio assessment	Application of mathematical tools to engineered products and engineering services.

Or

Optional Units (Block C)

Engineering in Business and the Environment	portfolio assessment	Structure of engineering companies. Combination of commercial and engineering functions. Environmental issues affecting the engineering industry.
Application of New Technology in Engineering	portfolio assessment	The main fields of new technology. Exploration of application in products and services.

And two units from:

Optional Units (Block D)

A choice of over 18 units with titles such as *Communications Engineering, Electronics, Engineering Drawings, Computer Aided Drawing, Vehicle Engine Technology* and *Telecommunications Technology.*

Moving on

Combined with other A-levels, the Vocational A-level in Engineering can lead to courses and careers in:

- Electrical Engineering
- Product Design
- Manufacturing Engineering.

HEALTH & SOCIAL CARE

Compulsory Units (Block A)

Equal Opportunities & Client Rights	externally assessed	Ethical issues associated with work in care and early years' environments. Implementation of equal opportunities legislation.
Communicating in Health & Social Care	portfolio assessed	Effective communication and evaluation of communication. Importance and protection of confidentiality.
Factors Affecting Human Growth & Development	externally assessed	Development from birth to death. Theories of development. Influences of genetic and environmental factors.

Optional Units (Block B)

At least one of the following:

Physical Aspects of Health	portfolio assessed	Record measurements of bodily functions. Interaction of systems to maintain health.
Health, Social Care & Early Years' Services	portfolio assessed	Origins and development of the services. National and local provision. Organisation and funding. The role of informal carers.

Optional Units (Block C)

One or two units from a choice of 20 including such titles as *Child Development, Social Policy, Physiological Disorders, Cell Structure, Genetics and Reproduction for Health Care, Child Care Practice* and *Influences on Health & Disease.*

Moving on

Combined with other A-levels, the Vocational A-level in Health & Social Care can lead to courses and careers in:

- Nursing

- Midwifery

- Teacher Training

- Social Work

- Social Science.

HOSPITALITY & CATERING

Compulsory Units (Block A)

The Hospitality & Catering Industry	externally assessed	The scale and scope of the industry. Investigation of organisations and outlets in different sectors.
Safety, Security & the Environment	externally assessed	Management of safety, the safety of food, security and the environment in hospitality and catering outlets.

Optional Units (Block B)

At least one of the following:

Food & Drink Operations	portfolio assessed	Understanding of food and drink operations. Investigate and observe preparation, cooking and service systems and evaluation of effectiveness.

Accommodation & Front Office Operations	portfolio assessed	Their role in different outlets. Research, compare and evaluate different outlets.

Optional Units (Block C)

Two or three units taken from a choice of 17 options including titles such as *Customer Service, Purchasing Costing and Control, On-Licensed Trade Operations, Event Supervision, International Hospitality and Personnel and Training for Hospitality & Catering.*

Moving on

Combined with other A-levels, the Vocational A-level in Hospitality & Catering can lead to courses and careers in:

- Food and Beverage Operations
- Front of House
- Accommodation Services
- Conference and Banqueting
- Trainee Management.

INFORMATION & COMMUNICATION TECHNOLOGY

Compulsory Units (Block A)

Presenting Information	portfolio assessment	Create original documents. Understand how organisations present and gather information and why standard layouts are used.
ICT Serving Organisations	external assessment	How organisations are structured. Use and exchange of information. Evaluation of ICT systems in organisations.
Spreadsheet Design	portfolio assessment	Design spreadsheets to process data. Prepare standard spreadsheets. Develop a working specification. Use spreadsheet facilities to develop, test and present information. Develop user documentation.

Optional Units (Block B)

Three units from a choice of 21 including both external and portfolio assessment. Titles include *Systems Analysis, Database Design, Multimedia, The Internet: Systems & Services, The Human-Computer Interface, Artificial Intelligence & Knowledge-based Systems.*

Moving on

Combined with other A-levels, a Vocational A-level in Information & Communication Technology can lead to a university course or employment in the following areas:

- Computer-based courses

- Communications

- Media

- Business

- Management

- Programming

- Systems Analysis

- Multimedia

- Software Systems

- Project Management

- Hardware Applications.

LEISURE & RECREATION

Compulsory Units (Block A)

Investigating Leisure & Recreation	portfolio assessment	Understand the industry, its structure and scale, the range of products, services and employment opportunities.
Safe Working Practice in the Leisure & Recreation Industry	external assessment	Health & safety and security responsibilities. Laws and regulations. Management plans for safe and secure environments. Risk assessment.

The Sports Industry	portfolio assessment	The structure, economic impact, organisation and funding of the industry. Sport and the mass media. Current trends in sport.
Marketing in Leisure & Recreation	external assessment	The marketing process. Identification and meeting of customer needs.
Customer Service in Leisure & Recreation	portfolio assessment	The importance of customer service. Customer service in a variety of situations with a variety of customers. The effectiveness of customer service in different organisations.

Optional Units (Block B)

One unit from a choice of 18 including both external and portfolio assessment. Titles include *Exercise Physiology, Fitness Testing & Training, Sports Psychology, Countryside Recreation, Arts, Museums & Cultural Heritage, Visitor Attractions.*

Moving on

Combined with other A-levels,* a Vocational A-level in Leisure & Recreation can lead to a university course or employment in the following areas:

• Sports Science

• Recreation & Leisure Studies

• Recreational Management

• Leisure Activities

• Armed Forces.

* Leisure & Recreation should not be combined with Vocational A-level Travel & Tourism due to the degree of overlap.

MANUFACTURING

Compulsory Units

Production Planning & Costing	external assessment	Use of product design specification to produce a realistic production plan and schedule for manufacture. Cost of manufacture and calculation of selling price.

And either:

Health & Safety and Environmental Impact	portfolio assessment	Responsibilities for Health & Safety and environmental management. Environmental impacts of industry. Risk assessment.
Quality Assurance & Control	external assessment	Achievement of quality standards. Investigation of a local company.

Or:

Production, Creation and Development	portfolio assessment	Development of a product from initial customer requirement to specification for manufacture.
Manufacturing Products	portfolio assessment	The opportunity to make products. Demonstrate the ability to repeat operations to quality standards.

Optional Units

Three from a choice of 19 including both external and portfolio assessment. Titles include *Marketing, Physical Science, Global Manufacturing, Biological Manufacturing, Robot Technology, Product Packaging* and *Computer Aided Design for Manufacturing.*

Moving on

Combined with other A-levels, the Vocational A-level in Manufacturing can lead to courses and careers in:

- Manufacturing

- Engineering

- Material Science

- Industrial Design

- Product Design

- Computer Aided Design

- Business

- Management.

MEDIA: COMMUNICATION & PRODUCTION

Compulsory Units

Analyse Media Products	external assessment	How media texts such as newspapers, TV and film work. Understanding of decisions made by producers and audience recognition of conventions.
Skills Development	portfolio assessment	Practice and develop media production skills. Develop creative, technical and evaluative skills in a particular area of media production. Self-assessment of skills and the need for future development.
Media Industries	external assessment	Investigation of a range of media industries. Understanding of the organisation of the sector. Range of media companies and products available.

Optional Units (Block B)

Three units from a choice of 22 including both portfolio and external assessment. Titles include *Produce a Media Product, Media Marketing, Writing to a Commission, Sound Recording Techniques, Radio Drama Production, Animating Images, Multimedia Technology, Freelance Work* and *Music Recording*.

Moving on

Combined with other A-levels, a Vocational A-level in Media can lead to a university course or employment in the following areas:

- Performing Arts
- Media and Film Studies
- Art-based degree courses.

PERFORMING ARTS

Compulsory Units (Block A)

Investigating Performing Arts Industry	external assessment	The performances, events, variety and technical services offered by the industry.
Skills Development	portfolio assessment	Skill building in at least one of six specialisms: Administration & marketing, dance, drama, music, music technology and technical aspects of performance.
Performing Work	portfolio assessment	Putting on a performance as a performer and as a member of a production team.

Optional Units

Three from a choice of 22 including both external and portfolio assessment. Titles include *Creating Work for a Performance, Working in Performing Arts, Movement Skills, Jazz Dance, Devising Drama, Keyboard Skills, Recording, Stage Managing a Performance, Theatre Design, Box Office & Front of House.*

Moving on

Combined with other A-levels, the Vocational A-level in Performing Arts can lead to courses and careers in:

- Performing Arts
- Combined Arts
- Dance

- Music

- Arts Administration.

RETAIL & DISTRIBUTIVE SERVICES

Compulsory Units

Developments in Retail & Distributive Services	portfolio assessment	Overview of services. The changing nature of retail and distributive services.
Finance for Retail & Distributive Services	portfolio assessment	Collection, use and management of financial information. Making a profit. Storing, displaying and selling goods.
Customer Service	external assessment	Meeting customer needs. Quality and quality assurance linked to customer care.

Optional Units

Three from a choice of 13 including both external and portfolio assessment. Titles include *Visual Merchandising, Distribution of Goods, Stock Management, IT in Distribution, Fashion Retailing, International Distribution* and *Personal Selling.*

Moving on

Combined with other A-levels, the Vocational A-level in Retail & Distributive Services can lead to courses and careers in:

- Retail

- Distribution

- Business

- Retail Management

- Merchandising

- Buying

- Fashion

- Marketing

- Advertising
- Display
- Stock Management
- Distribution Management
- Sales Management
- Key Account Management
- Logistics.

SCIENCE

Compulsory Units (Block A)

Investigating Science at Work	portfolio assessed	Use of science. Investigating organisations such as pharmaceutical companies, farms and hospitals. Their functions, methods and products.
Carrying out Scientific nvestigation	portfolio assessed	Investigation skills. Carry out investigations. Science, communication and management in the science industry.

Optional Units (Block B)

Two of the following:

Monitoring the Activity of the Human Body	externally assessed	How the body works. Monitoring and measuring fitness. Response to different conditions including exercise.
Controlling Chemical Processes	externally assessed	Manufacture of a variety of chemical compounds, eg dyes and medicines. Control of manufacturing processes for safety, effectiveness and profitability.
Controlling the Transfer of Energy	externally assessed	Types of energy. Their costs and efficiencies. Environmental and energy conservation issues.

Optional Units (Block C)

Two from a choice of 22, including both portfolio and external assessment. Titles include; *Genetic Engineering, Chemical Detectives, Putting Chemicals to Work, Using Maths in Science, Medical Physics, Disease and Diagnosis, Medical Microbiology, Animal Management* and *Managing Natural Resources.*

Moving on

Combined with other A-levels, the Vocational A-level in Science can lead to courses and careers in:

• Nursing

• Environment

• Biotechnology

• Chemical Analysis

• Food Technology

• Engineering.

TRAVEL & TOURISM

Compulsory Units

Investigating Travel & Tourism	portfolio assessed	An understanding of the industry. Organisations, products and services. The significance to the UK economy and employment.
Tourism Development	externally assessed	Impact on the industry. Organisations involved. The management of tourism development.
Worldwide Travel Destinations	portfolio assessed	Major continental and long haul destinations, their locations and key features. Attraction to different tourist groups.
Marketing in Travel & Tourism	externally assessed	The marketing process. Identification and meeting of customer needs. Methods of communication.

| Customer Service in | portfolio | The importance of excellence. |
| Travel & Tourism | assessed | The opportunity to provide customer service in different organisations. |

Optional Units

One unit from a choice of 17 including both external and portfolio assessment. Titles include *UK Travel Destinations, Tour Operations, Working as an Overseas Representative, Visitor Attractions, Arts, Museums and Cultural Heritage, Countryside Recreation.*

Moving on

Combined with other A-levels*, a Vocational A-level in Travel & Tourism can lead to a university course or employment in the following areas:

- Travel & Tourism Management

- Marketing

- Tour Operations

- Airlines

- Business Travel.

* Travel & Tourism should not be combined with Vocational A-level Leisure & Recreation due to the degree of overlap.

Section 3

A-level subjects

Choosing your A-level subjects

There is always a danger that a guide like this may create more confusion and dilemma than it removes; for you may have been unaware of many of the subjects that are available at A-level until you saw the list on pages 35–37. This is all the more reason for a good strategy in making up your mind about which are the ones for you.

There is no fail-safe formula that can provide the right answer for everyone. Like all decisions, this one has to be reached by achieving a balance between a number of different, and sometimes conflicting, considerations. The strategy we propose consists of asking yourself four questions and undertaking four tasks.

THE QUESTIONS

What subjects are available?
Few schools or colleges offer all the A-level subjects listed in this guide. Even if the subjects you choose are on the curriculum at the institution you attend, there is no guarantee that you will be able to study all of them since the timetable can make some combinations of subjects impossible to pursue. The first question to ask is what is available at the school or college you attend or one to which you could move.

What subjects do I like?
Instinct may be as good a guide as any to A-level choice. You will perform best and get the best results when you are enjoying your work and are fully committed to it. If you make your choice purely out of a sense of duty, or because of external pressure, you are unlikely to make the most of a subject.

Nevertheless, remember that you may not be able to say if you like a subject until you have tried it. It is in the sixth form that many students discover their potential in new areas and develop interests and enthusiasms that last a lifetime.

What am I good at?

Interest in a subject must be matched by the necessary ability. Before embarking on a course, you need to ask yourself whether you have the appropriate skills. If you cannot perform to an adequate standard you are likely to lose interest and confidence. All arts subjects at A-level help to develop powers of expression and it would be a mistake to choose such subjects without a good, proven standard of English. Similarly, it would not be realistic to choose some sciences, or Economics, without a secure mathematical foundation. In many cases the best people to advise here are your teachers, who will be able to assess your ability and are familiar with the demands of different subjects. GCSE grades are also a good, though not an infallible guide.

What A-level subjects do I need?

You may not need any particular subjects; but many college or university departments do have specific requirements. For instance, if you want to be a doctor or a vet, you will need at least two science subjects. For an Economics degree you will often need Mathematics. A list of university subjects, and the A-levels often required for admission to study them, is given on page 84.

THE TASKS

Talk to teachers who know you

This can be one of the most useful and important things you can do. A teacher who knows what different A-levels demand *and* who knows your strengths and weaknesses is uniquely well placed to advise you. You may not agree with the advice; but you should hear it.

Talk also to those who teach any A-level subject you are considering, even if they don't know you particularly well. It is always best to hear from the person responsible for teaching a subject what it is like and what it involves.

Talk to other students

Talking to other students, only a little older than you, who have themselves studied a subject you are considering, can be very instructive. However, you must learn to evaluate what will be very subjective views and realise that what is important for someone else may not be so for you.

Attend open days

Open days or evenings run by schools and colleges can be an excellent way of learning about different A-level subjects and what is involved in studying them.

Read the textbooks

It is always a good idea to read some of the books which you will be required to study as part of any A-level course. Don't choose these yourself: ask the person who is likely to be teaching the subject for some recommendations.

POINTS TO REMEMBER

Distinguish between the teacher and the subject

You may like or dislike a subject because of a particular teacher or because of how it is taught at your school or college. This may be a good reason for choosing a subject; but it may not. If you are influenced by such considerations, try to find out whether the teacher in question is likely to be teaching you and if so, for how long.

A-levels not only impart knowledge; they develop skills

When choosing your A-level subjects don't just think about the subject matter of the A-level — whether you like the idea of learning historical facts, the laws of motion, a foreign language. Consider also what *skills* you will be asked to acquire and whether you like the sound of them. Many subjects require and develop the ability to analyse abstract arguments and to formulate your own in essay form; others require the ability to solve mathematical and scientific problems; some require you to memorise facts and figures; others demand practical skills; a few require artistic and creative talents — visual, dramatic, musical. At the same time, do not be put off by claims that certain subjects require sophisticated skills which you feel you don't already have. The only requirement is that you have the capacity to *develop* those skills. After all, if you had them already, you probably wouldn't need to pursue the A-level course in the first place.

THE ISSUE OF RELEVANCE

Today everyone demands that their education should be relevant. Do not be misled by misguided views about relevance. All A-levels are 'relevant', not because they *train* you for particular jobs or careers, but because they *develop skills* which are required for them all. The titles of the subjects may differ, but they all share the same general objectives: to teach you how to find, sift and evaluate information; how to analyse problems and construct possible solutions; how to present a well-argued case orally or on paper; how to cope with complexity.

The idea that specific subjects are 'relevant' to specific careers is a dangerous one. Even at a higher level, most degree courses at universities and colleges are not directly vocational in this sense – though there are obvious exceptions such as Medicine, Engineering and Architecture. There are hundreds of Chemistry graduates, for instance, who have made their careers in business, politics, law or administration (a notable example being our last Prime Minister). The answers to the questions a chemist asks are rarely ones which allow for a simple answer – and so Chemistry can be a good training for dealing with a complex world. And it is not only 'arts' students who learn something about expression and communication.

It is even more dangerous to look for narrow 'relevance' at sixth-form level. A-level Law, for instance, may not necessarily be the best choice for a student who is thinking of the law as a career. Law is a fascinating subject which deals with the application of general rules to particular situations and raises fundamental questions of political, social and moral importance. The student of Law, like the student of Chemistry, has to learn how to turn mess into order, how to find provisional solutions to insoluble problems, how to make the best of a difficult job. To that extent, Law is a subject which is 'relevant' to all students. But those whose sights are set on the law as a career might be better advised to study, in the sixth form, English Literature, Mathematics or Economics, in order to lay firm foundations for their future legal studies. The lawyer who knows only the law is not likely to be good at his or her job. A purely utilitarian education makes for a dull human being.

Do I need the GCSE?

A few A-level subjects cannot sensibly be studied unless you have already taken and probably passed the GCSE in the same subject. Many others, however, can be studied from scratch.

Those subjects which should only be attempted if you have passed a GCSE in the same subject are listed below – but remember there are no hard and fast rules. If a GCSE is declared to be essential it is usually possible to start the A-level without it provided you are willing to make up the missed material while preparing for the A-level.

What is much more important is your *overall* GCSE performance, in particular how you fared in Mathematics and English Language. In fact, your performance *in these two subjects and your five best other GCSE subjects* is a better indicator of how you are likely to do in a particular A-level subject than your performance in that subject alone.

GCSE important

Subjects for which *the same* GCSE is essential or desirable:

Art & Design	Greek
Biology (Chemistry also important)	Latin
Chemistry	Mathematics
English Language	Modern Languages
Environmental Science/Studies	Music
	Physics (Maths also important)

Mathematics GCSE desirable

Subjects which may be studied at A-level without a GCSE in the same subject, but for which Mathematics GCSE is highly desirable:

Accounting	Economics
Business Studies	Geology
Computer Studies	Psychology

English Language GCSE desirable

Subjects which may be studied at A-level without a GCSE in the same subject, but for which English Language GCSE is highly desirable:

Ancient History	History of Art
Classical Studies	Media Studies
Communication Studies	Philosophy
English Literature	Politics
General Studies	Religious Studies
Geography	Sociology
History	Theatre Studies

What are A-levels useful for?

Education has always paid homage to two gods, to the 'higher' callings of philosophical and speculative thought and creative activity as well as to the dictates of the practical world requiring the three Rs – Reading, 'Riting and 'Rithmetic. Teachers show us how to think and to extend the frontiers of knowledge and understanding (without always knowing where our thoughts will lead us). They also aim to show us how to acquire more practical skills and how to survive in everyday life.

In the current atmosphere it is the practical and utilitarian role of education which has gained the upper hand. Education is packaged into courses and syllabuses, each designed to 'lead' somewhere, to provide entry into another course or to provide training for a job. 'Relevance' is the key word.

However, A-levels were originally intended to foster important intellectual skills and to develop the capacity for abstract, analytical and creative thought, without regard to short-term practical objectives. Although these aims are still considered, A-levels are increasingly seen as just practical exercises and qualifications – the means by which we may obtain a place at university or entry to a profession, or as a route to employment.

Higher education

In order to obtain a place at a university to study for a degree you will need either two or three A-levels, depending on the course for which you are applying. For the more competitive courses it won't be sufficient just to pass the A-levels: you will need to obtain good grades as well. (Your will also need to have passed some GCSEs.) Furthermore, some courses require specific subjects. Thus, if you want to study medicine, at least two of your A-levels must be sciences.

If you wish to read Economics at university, it is a good idea to study Mathematics at A-level. The table below lists the main degree courses and the subjects that are usually required or preferred.

For entry to other courses in higher education, such as a Higher National Diploma or a Diploma of Higher Education, one A-level may be enough. In order to find out the A-level or AS-level requirements for these courses of study, you must consult the prospectus of each institution. The information is summarised in *The Official Guide to University and College Entrance* published by UCAS.

Entry to a profession

Each profession has its own rules governing entry. Most professional bodies these days recruit mainly from among applicants with university or college degrees. A few admit school-leavers. In both cases, you will almost certainly need A-levels.

Employment

There are many jobs for which A-levels are neither required nor indeed relevant or desirable. Nevertheless, there are many which do require the aptitude and level of education of which A-levels are an indicator; and having one or two of them can make a significant difference to your chances of employment.

Subject required or preferred for university/college degrees or careers

Degree/career	A-level subjects
Accountancy	*Usually any; sometimes Maths; not Accounting*
African, Asian, Oriental languages	*Classical or modern language*
Agriculture	*Chemistry; sometimes Biology or both*
American Studies	*English Literature*
Archaeology	*Any subject; science an advantage*
Architecture	*Usually none; sometimes Maths or Physics*
Art	*Art & Design*

Degree/career	A-level subjects
Art History	*None; any suitable arts subject*
Biochemistry	*Chemistry & either one or two of Biology, Maths, Physics*
Business Studies	*Sometimes Maths*
Chemistry	*Chemistry & Maths or Physics*
Classical Studies	*Any suitable arts subject*
Communication Studies	*Any subject*
Computer Science	*Maths*
Dentistry	*Chemistry & two sciences*
Drama	*Arts subjects; English an advantage*
Economics	*Often Maths*
Education	*Any subject*
Engineering – Aeronautical	*Maths & Physics*
Engineering – Chemistry	*Maths & Chemistry*
Engineering – Civil	*Maths or Maths & Physics*
Engineering – Electrical	*Maths & Physics*
Engineering – General	*Maths & Physics*
Engineering – Mechanical	*Maths & Physics*
English Literature	*English Literature*
Environmental Studies	*Any two sciences*
French	*French*
Geography	*Geography*
Geology	*Maths & Physics or any two sciences*
German	*German*
Greek	*Greek*
History	*Any arts subject; History an advantage*
Italian	*Italian*
Latin	*Latin*
Law	*Any subject*
Mathematics	*Maths & sometimes Further Maths*
Media Studies	*Any subject*

Medicine	*Chemistry, Biology, Physics or Maths*
Music	*Music*
Nursing	*Sometimes one science*
Occupational Therapy	*Any subject*
Pharmacology	*Chemistry & one or two sciences*
Pharmacy	*Chemistry & one or two sciences*
Philosophy	*Any subject*
Physics	*Physics & Maths*
Physiology	*Chemistry & two other sciences*
Physiotherapy	*One or two sciences*
Politics	*Any social science or arts subject*
Psychology	*Any subject, often Maths or a science*
Russian	*Russian*
Sociology	*Any social science or arts subject*
Spanish	*Spanish*
Statistics	*Maths*
Theatre	*Any arts subject; occasionally English*
Theology	*Any arts subject*
Veterinary Science	*Chemistry, Biology & Physics or Maths*

A-level subjects

In the pages that follow, the descriptions of each A-level are designed to give an idea of what it is like to study that subject; they should not be taken as an accurate account of any particular A-level syllabus. Remember that a given A-level subject is usually set by several or all of the exam boards, and subject matter that forms part of one syllabus (compulsorily or as an option) may not be found in another. In order to find out about the syllabus of a particular examining board, you must consult the syllabus booklet issued by the board itself.

Course information provided

Requirements
Lists the skills and aptitudes required and indicates whether the GCSE in the same subject is required or not.

Goes well with
Suggests the most suitable or most usual, but by no means the only possible subjects that may be studied in tandem.

Higher education suitability
Lists the conventional university courses which are based on or require the subject.

Suggested reading
Lists books you could read in order to discover more about the subject.

Arts & Humanities

ACCOUNTING

The maintenance of financial records and their presentation to suit particular purposes — be it the demands of the tax collector, an enquiry from the bank manager or the agenda of a company's Annual General Meeting — is something few of us can now escape. One of the legacies of the Thatcher era has been the application to almost all areas of life, from education to medicine, of the principles of the marketplace, the cornerstone of which is good financial information. The last quarter of the 20th century may well be seen as the era of the accountant.

Legend has it that it was the needs of prosperous Italian traders that led to the foundation and growth of many accounting practices that are still with us today. The enterprises of these traders were more complex than those of their predecessors and required a system of determining trading gain or loss that was more sophisticated than the cumbersome process of counting precious coins in the till. Paper transactions and records were found more efficient in time but they gave rise to the need to be able to 'prove' a relationship between a profit on paper and money in the bank. The answer was double-entry bookkeeping, a practice that still lies at the heart of most contemporary financial accounting systems.

There is, however, little evidence of much professional accountancy in Europe until the 19th century. In England it received a great impetus from the growth of limited liability companies, which from 1850 onwards both accompanied and led to the growth of business operations on a scale hitherto unknown. It was the need for proper control of these operations, and the growth of multiple ownership, which the company system made possible, that called for the wider use of more sophisticated accounting and auditing systems. The Institute of Accountants was formed in London in 1870 and was incorporated by Royal Charter ten years later.

Accountants, even in these early days, had two principal functions: first, to prepare financial statements of trading activity; and second, to act as independent auditors (verifiers) of this task. Today, trained accountants undertake these traditional tasks but also very many others. They advise individuals and companies about their tax liabilities. They act as company secretaries. They use their accountancy knowledge in order to run their own businesses or to act as financial directors in other enterprises. They are a versatile and employable breed.

Subject criteria

There are no QCA subject criteria for Accounting at A-level. The following unit titles are available for study.

AS

The Accounting information system

Introduction to published accounts

Financial Accounting

Introduction to management Accounting

Accounting principles

Final accounts

A2

Management Accounting

Company accounts & interpretation

Further aspects of financial Accounting

Published accounts of limited companies

Coursework

Assessment of A-level Accounting is by written examination only.

Course Information

Requirements

GCSE maths at grade C or above.

Goes well with

Social sciences such as Law, Politics or Economics, and Mathematics.

Higher education suitability

Not universally accepted, even as a third A-level, and particularly not for an Accounts degree: check before applying with this A-level.

Suggested reading

R. Izhar. *Accounting, Costing & Management*. OUP
H. Randall. *A Level Accounting*. Letts
F. Woods & A. Sangster. *Business Accounting*. FT/Pitman
F. Woods. *A Level Accounting*. FT/Pitman

ANCIENT HISTORY

Ancient History is the study of two corners of the world between approximately two and six thousand years ago: Greece and Rome, together with the empires that grew from them. These empires were neither the first nor the last in world history; but they had an extraordinary influence on the subsequent development of western civilisation. The European Renaissance that ended the Middle Ages was deeply rooted in this ancient heritage, as the influence of Platonic and Aristotelian ideas, classical art and architecture, Roman law and Athenian democracy demonstrate.

Greece

The 5th century BC saw a rapid flowering of philosophy and intellectual activity of an intensity rarely encountered elsewhere in any epoch. It also saw the emergence of Athens as an imperial power as it formed and led the Delian League, opposed by Sparta's Peloponnesian League. The rivalry between Athens and Sparta was to culminate between 431 and 404 BC in a conflict known as the Peloponnesian Wars, and the eventual defeat of Athens. The 4th century then saw a series of shifting alliances between Athens, Sparta and neighbouring Thebes and Corinth, all of whom were to fall prey to Philip of Macedon, whose son Alexander extended his empire to Egypt, Persia and India.

Rome

Rome in its early days was ruled by kings. However, in 510 BC a Republic was founded. From that point Rome started on the gradual road that led to its total control of the Mediterranean and beyond. In a series of engagements, known as the Punic Wars, the Romans eventually defeated the Carthaginian leader Hannibal, and emerged in 202 BC as a major power.

The republican system struggled to cope with the problems caused by its sudden acquisition of wealth and international power. Rome became gradually ungovernable, until eventually Caesar emerged in 45 BC with dictatorial powers. His murder by the traditionalists two years later provoked a further period of civil war. His successor, Octavian, ruled for 45 years, under the new title of Augustus; he transformed the political system into a centralised monarchy and extended the boundaries of empire.

The advent of Nerva in 96 AD heralded a new system whereby the emperor adopted as his successor a man of tested ability, and the following four emperors – Trajan, Hadrian, Antoninus Pius and Marcus Aurelius (96–180 AD) – presided over the most prosperous and efficient era of Roman history. If the Roman Empire 'declined', it took a long time to do so and the reasons for that decline are still hotly debated by historians. The last Roman emperor was deposed by the Goths in 476 AD.

Ancient History is offered by a single awarding body: OCR. The specification complies with the subject criteria for History that are listed below; it is designed to offer students a choice of topics in Greek and Roman history from the 6th century BC to the 4th century AD.

Subject criteria

AS & A2

Develop an understanding of historical terms and contexts

Explore the significance of events, individuals, ideas, attitudes, beliefs, issues and societies

Understand the nature of historical evidence and methods used in analysis and evaluation

Understand and analyse interpretation and representation of historical events

Study a range of historical perspectives, eg cultural, economic and political

Analyse, evaluate, interpret and use historical sources

Use a range of historical concepts in an appropriate manner

A2

Study the history of one or more country/state

Study change over a period of time, both long and short term

Draw comparisons between different aspects of the period, society, theme or topic studied

Investigate specific historical questions, problems or issues

Use historical sources, accounts, arguments and interpretations to explain, analyse, synthesise and make judgements

Content

Greek History: Herodotus on Persia. The Athenian Empire. The trial of Socrates. The conflict of Greece and Persia. Greek History 446–413 BC. The Culture of Athens. The Culture of Tyranny 600–479 BC. Sparta in the Greek World. Athenian Democracy.

Roman History: The Catilinarian Conspiracy. Augustus and Augustan Propaganda. Nero. Roman History 81–44 BC. The Age of Augustus. Roman History AD 14–68. The Growth and Government of the Roman Empire. The City of Rome. Emperors and Empire.

Roman World: Britain through Roman Eyes. Julian. Roman Britain AD 43–160. Diocletian and Constantine. The Romanisation of Britain. The Christianising of the Roman Empire.

Coursework

As an alternative to Unit 5 (Advanced thematic study) A2 candidates may choose to be assessed on an individual study (Unit 7) either from a list drawn up by the board or of their own choice. The coursework element comprises 16.7% of the total marks. There is no coursework element in the specification for AS.

Course information

Requirements

Students who have previously studied History or Humanities at GCSE are likely to be expected to have achieved grade C or above

Goes well with

Any combination of arts subjects, also Latin and Greek

Higher education suitability

Any humanities degree, especially English, History, Ancient History, Classical Civilisation, History of Art

Suggested reading

J. Alcock. *Life in Roman Britain*. English Heritage/Batsford
A.R. Burn. *Persia & the Greeks*. Duckworth
J.M. Cook. *The Persian Empire*. Dent
C. Edwards. *Writing Rome. Textual Approaches to the City*. CUP

ARCHAEOLOGY

There are no longer any blank spaces left to be filled in on the world map; there are other worlds, however, waiting to be discovered – those that lie beneath our feet, the buried civilisations of the past. The exploration and reconstruction of these civilisations is the province of the archaeologist.

Archaeology (from the Greek *archaeos* = ancient, and *logos* = study) was pioneered in the 18th century by enthusiastic antiquarians. In the early 19th century a more systematic approach to the subject was developed, mainly by British and Danish scholars, who began to map out the vast time span of pre-history. They invented the terms 'Stone Age', 'Bronze Age' and 'Iron Age' to mark successive stages of human development based on the materials used for tools and weapons. Darwin's theory of evolution had momentous consequences for the study of the remote past.

Well before the First World War archaeology had passed from the hands of amateurs into those of professionals, and over the last 70 years it has been completely transformed. The identification of sites for excavation previously relied on chance discoveries made by the ploughman or the builder, but the modern archaeologist can call on the assistance of aerial photography, ground-penetrating radar, and even the remote sensing of orbiting satellites. More sophisticated dating techniques are now available, such as radiocarbon analysis and dendrochronology (tree-dating). Modern archaeologists not only dig, they dive: sonar and electronic sensing have brought whole new underwater worlds to light. Recent years have also seen the advent of 'Rescue Archaeology', as motorway and inner-city development have uncovered hitherto inaccessible sites that have to be investigated by emergency teams working against the clock. The chance discovery of a hidden hoard may catch the public imagination from time to time and become front-page news, but major advances are the result of years of patient, systematic and often frustrating searching. The archaeologist has to combine the skill and patience of the scientist with the creative imagination of the historian.

Archaeology in the late 20th century is a multidisciplinary science that draws on the findings and techniques of many different areas of study. History, however, is still its closest relation. For many periods of human history, in the absence of written records, archaeology is our only key to the past; and even when written records survive, archaeology adds flesh to their bones.

Subject criteria

There are no QCA subject criteria for Archaeology at A-level. The following unit titles are available for study.

AS

Archaeological sources & methods: Survey and excavation

Archaeological sources & methods: Post-excavation, dating and interpretation

Religion & ritual

A2

Settlement & social organisation

Material culture, technology & economics

Options

The following are available as options within Religion and ritual:

- Prehistoric Britain (Neolithic to Iron Age)
- Ancient Egypt
- The Roman World
- The Maya.

Coursework

The AQA syllabus includes a compulsory personal study with a focus on a local environment and archaeological methodology.

Course information

Requirements

GCSE English and History at grade C or above likely to be preferred.

Goes well with

Historical subjects; environmental and human sciences.

Higher education suitability

Degree courses in Ancient and Medieval History.

Suggested reading
K. Greene. *Archaeology: An Introduction.* Batsford
P. Bahn (ed). *Dictionary of Archaeology.* Harper Collins

ART

Art refers simply to human skill (as opposed to natural skill) though it has come to be used to describe all forms of creative activity. The term 'design' refers to the compositional structure on which the visual arts depend.
Art is also used in the narrower sense of just painting and drawing – probably among the earliest forms of artistic enterprise engaged in by men and women. Palaeolithic paintings on cave walls are proof, even so early in human evolution, of the desire to create.

Decorative arts are the (design-based) arts concerned with the decoration of functional objects: architectural units, furniture, textiles, a pot or a mirror. Good decorative art is appropriate in its adaptation and seems to be part of the object on which it is executed, as though it had sprung from within rather than having been applied to the surface.

Sculpture: Sculptors work in different ways, with many materials. They may carve directly from hard materials such as stone or marble to produce what is known as a piece of 'subtractive' sculpture; or use softer materials, such as clay, to build up a piece of 'constructive' sculpture.

Graphic design is the exploitation of artistic skills for practical ends – usually of a presentational nature. It includes poster-making, calligraphy (lettering), creating logos and book illustration.

Ceramics is the art of working in clay, whether as sculpture, modelling or pot-making. As in many artistic activities, imagination and creativity are expressed through technical expertise.

Textiles: Fabrics themselves may be created in many ways (woven, spun, knitted, etc); their patterns and colours may be 'intrinsic' through such means as the selected use of wools and cottons, or 'extrinsic' as is the case with needlework, embroidery or printing on silk. Those working in this field may need to learn, among other things, about the techniques of fabric production, and dyes, chemical and natural.

Photography is regarded by some as not an art at all – partly because of the belief that the camera slavishly copies the world in front of it and partly because it is seen as a process requiring no hand-eye coordination. Nevertheless, the photograph is the product of human determination; it demonstrates very clearly, by means of its technical apparatus that life takes the shape determined for it by the beholder.

Almost all artists are influenced consciously or unconsciously by their predecessors, and many will wish to study the history of their art in a thorough and systematic way at some stage. The history of art is discussed at greater length on page 157.

Subject criteria

AS

Integrated critical, practical and theoretical study in Art, Craft & Design including first-hand experience of original works

A2

Builds on AS allowing for greater depth of study

Might be achieved by:

- greater specialisation in a particular medium/process

- extended development of particular themes/ideas

- further theoretical research

- more rigorous exploration of an inter-disciplinary or multi-disciplinary approach

Common to AS & A2

Knowledge and understanding of:

- materials, processes, technologies and resources

- conveyance of ideas, feelings and meanings and their interpretation in images and artefacts

- relation of images and artefacts to the time and place in which they are made and to social and cultural contexts

- continuity and change in different genres, styles and traditions

- A working vocabulary and specialist terminology

- Recording experiences and observations, research techniques

- Exploration of relevant resources, analytical and evaluation skills

- Use of knowledge and understanding of the work of others

- Generation and exploration of lines of enquiry

- Application of knowledge and understanding in making images and artefacts

- Organisation, selection and communication of ideas, solutions and responses in a range of visual forms

AS and A-level Art courses are offered as a general (or *unendorsed*) programme or allow specialisation in a number of areas. Examples of these are listed under *Options*.

Options

- Art

- Fine Art (drawing and painting, sculpture, printmaking)

- Graphic Design (communication, computer graphics, illustration, advertising, film, video, television)

- Textiles (printing, tie-dye, batik, spraying and transfer, appliqué, patchwork, padding, quilting, weaving and knitting)

- 3D-Design (ceramics, body ornament, theatre design, exhibition design and display, interior design and product design)

- Photography (practical, critical, contextual work with images created by chemical and/or digital means)

- Critical & Contextual Studies in Art (methods of artists, designers, critics and art historians; style and meaning in art, architecture, craft and design).

Coursework

All specifications include 60% coursework. Individual specifications vary as to the style of this. Examples include enquiries on particular themes, contextual study, problem solving and independent study.

Course Information

Requirements

Where GCSE has been taken prior to commencement of the course, a pass at grade C or above will be expected; some centres may ask for a portfolio of work at interview.

Goes well with

Any subject other than Art History.

Higher education suitability

Important for art- and design-related courses, History of Art, Architecture; may not be accepted as an academic A-level for some degree courses.

Suggested reading
E.H. Gombrich. *The Story of Art*. Phaidon
H. Honor & J. Fleming. *A World History of Art*. Thames & Hudson
H.W. Janson. *History of Art for Young People*. Thames & Hudson

BIOLOGICAL SCIENCE

Biology

Biology is the study of the living world, encompassing study of the anatomy and physiology of humans and animals, their lifestyles and habits; and of plant life in all its forms. Biologists look at the conditions necessary for the continuity of life and for evolution.

On a simple level the biologist records the organic world we live in, describing the range and characteristics of animal and plant life (the shape of a skeleton, the reproductive life cycle of aphids, the number of recorded grasses). On a more sophisticated level the biologist explain animal behaviour (why do hedgehogs hibernate in winter, and how do they survive?), predicts its patterns (the annual migration of Canada geese), and asks questions about plant life (what are tropical rainforests and why are they important?). Further, the biologist establishes connections, not only between different species but between the human, animal and plant kingdoms themselves – in the process becoming an agriculturalist, horticulturalist or environmentalist.

Biology's claim to be the most important of the natural sciences today has much to do with the wide range of its applications and the many branches of our lives that it touches – from medicine to food production and from test-tube babies to genetic engineering. Indeed, the breadth of the subject is underlined by the many different 'biologies' there are.

Human Biology

Human Biology, as the term suggests, is the biology of men and women. Although only one of the main organisms to be found on the planet Earth, we have the means and ability to affect all other biological species from butterflies to blue whales. A sound understanding of *Homo sapiens* is thus more vital today than ever before. Not only have we created the agricultural environment we see around us; we are also busy destroying large portions of the life-support systems we rely on. Human Biology shows how plants make their food from carbon dioxide, water and sunlight, and how we are utterly dependent on these processes in order to feed ourselves.

Human biological studies also lie behind recent developments in modern medicine. Genetic engineering is opening up the possibility of detecting and treating many hitherto incurable diseases.

Finally, Human Biology is also concerned with our past. What is the evidence for our descent from the apes? Can we really trace tool-making skills back to over 2 million years ago; and what sort of organism made these tools? Would we be able to get on with our Neolithic ancestors? How did they organise their social structure?

Biological Science is offered as either Biology or Human Biology at A-level. The subject specifications include a number of common modules together with others, which are specific to the particular strand to be studied. Specific modules may be distinct as in the examples listed below or may be alternative versions of similar biological principles, eg *Exchange, transport and reproduction* (Biology) and *Exchange, transport and reproduction in humans* (Human Biology).

Both strands include material to enable compliance with the Biology subject criteria but specifications from different boards also allow the study of particular options.

Subject criteria

AS

Structure and role of biological molecules: carbohydrates, proteins and lipids; the importance of water and inorganic ions

The ultra-structure of cells and function of organelles, cell organisation to form tissues, tissues as components of organs

Structure and function of enzymes

Principles of mass transport and exchange at cell surfaces

Structural and physiological adaptation to the environment

DNA and RNA, protein synthesis, the gene–enzyme relationship

Cell division: mitosis and the conservation of genetic material

Energy flow in ecosystems

Factors affecting the stability of populations

Human impact on the environment

A2

The role of ATP and the processes of photosynthesis and respiration

Homeostasis: the maintenance of a constant and optimum internal environment

Coordination of response to stimuli: nervous and chemical

The inheritance of genetic material through meiosis and reproduction

Variation and diversity, the production of new species; the principles and importance of the classification of organisms

Options
Some optional modules are specific to Biology or Human Biology; some are common to either strand. Examples include:

- Making use of Biology (Biology)
- Physiology & the environment (Biology)
- Pathogens & disease (Human Biology)
- Reproduction, growth & ageing (Human Biology)
- Microbiology & biotechnology (common)
- Food science (common)
- Human health & fitness (common).

Coursework
Specifications all contain elements of practical coursework at both AS and A2 level. Examination boards differ in the way coursework is marked and/or moderated and also in the contribution made by this component to the total marks available. AQA specification A Biology/Biology (Human) as an example has all work marked by the teacher then moderated by the board. The coursework component makes up 30% of the AS and 25% of the A-level in this case.

Course Information

Requirements
Commonly at least one of the following GCSE subjects at grade C or above: Biology, Chemistry, Human Physiology & Health, Combined Science. GCSE Maths at C or above is a distinct advantage.

Goes well with
Any arts or science A-level, particularly Chemistry.

Higher education suitability
Both these A-levels are good preparation for a wide range of degrees; Biology/Human Biology is a requirement for many courses in the biological sciences, and is often preferred for Biochemistry, Pharmacy, Microbiology and Medicine.

> ### Suggested reading
> J. Adds, E. Larkcom and R. Miller. *Cell Biology and Genetics.* Nelson
> R. Leakey. *Origins.* Dai Nippon
> C. Clegg and D. Mackean. *Advanced Biology: Principles and Applications.* Murray
> N. Green, G. Stout and D. Taylor. *Biological Science.* Cambridge
> G. Tortora. *Principles of Anatomy and Physiology.* Harper and Row

BUSINESS STUDIES

One might be forgiven for assuming that whatever is taught in a programme of work called Business Studies is best learned in the university of the real world rather than in front of the blackboard, and that successful businessmen and women are formed by their experience of commerce rather than created by business schools. The fact is that our ever-increasing dependence on technical, acquired skills and knowledge has rendered such assumptions dangerously dated, and there is unquestionably a body of skills and knowledge that are just as important to the would-be entrepreneur, manager or captain of industry as motivation, judgement and luck. To illustrate the range of knowledge that a successful business might require, we will imagine a firm about to launch a new product, and list some of the questions that would have to be answered by its board of directors.

What type of business is it? What are the objectives of the firm? Who are its owners? Why is it located where it is? Why is it launching a new product? How has it decided whether there will be a demand? Where does it intend to sell it and why? How will it get it there? How did it decide on the design? Does the product meet legal requirements? How will the firm produce it? Where will it get its supplies from? What is to be the volume of production? How many workers does it need? How will they be organised? Are they to be skilled? What are the costs of producing? Will unions oppose any change in working practices? What price will the firm charge? How should it promote the product? What will its competitors do? How will consumers react? Will the business make a profit? What is the business planning to do next year and over the next five years?

Thus Business Studies involves areas as varied as Economics, Accounting, management studies, personnel, Computing, marketing, industrial relations and Law; it may also require a foreign language. It cannot avoid Government & Politics and Sociology: it deals with the internal and external influences on the behaviour and structure of an organisation. In addition, issues such as a firm's responsibilities to the community, the consumer, the government and its employees are examined. A businessman or woman with any experience will tell you that there is hardly an area of life their work does not touch upon.

However, Business Studies is not concerned with these subjects as separate disciplines: they may be learned separately, but they are only of use as components in a process that integrates all these skills and knowledge. Students must learn to think widely about issues and to understand that every situation in a business environment is unique and must be assessed in its own context.

Business Studies provides individuals with the necessary skills, knowledge and techniques to make effective business decisions.

In Business Studies there is no separation of topics between AS and A-level. A-level specifications develop higher level skills and extend the breadth and depth of knowledge and understanding.

Subject criteria

Objectives & the business environment: Business objectives, impact of external influences, business strategy

Marketing: Nature and role, market research, marketing plan, forecasting

Accounting & finance: Budgeting, balance sheets, cost analysis, investment appraisal factors

People in organisations: Human resource planning, management structure and organisation, motivation, employer/employee relations

Operations management: Operational efficiency, quality

Options

Unit titles closely follow the subject criteria above. Coursework is optional on A2 as below.

Coursework

None on AS. An optional assignment for A2 taken from a list supplied by the board. Alternatively a non-coursework option may be studied. The AQA coursework component is worth 15% of the total marks.

Course Information

Requirements

Maths and English Language GCSE at grade C or above may be required; grade C or above in GCSE Business Studies would be expected in those candidates who had previously studied the qualification.

Goes well with

Most subjects; especially Economics (but see Higher education suitability, below).

Higher education suitability

Acceptable for most courses. Candidates wishing to offer Business Studies with Accounting and/or Economics should check with their chosen HE institutions that the degree of overlap is not unacceptable.

Suggested reading

S. Danks. *Advanced Level Business Studies*. DP Publications
B. Jewell. *An Integrated Approach to Business Studies*. Longman
M. Surridge et al. *Finance, Information & Business*. Collins
J. Sutherland & D. Canwell. *Applied Business Series*. Hodder & Stoughton

CHEMISTRY

In the mid-19th century John Dalton put forward the revolutionary idea that all matter consisted of minute particles – invisible to the eye – which he called atoms. What is significant about Dalton's theory is not just the idea itself (the Greek philosopher, Democritus, had said something similar 2000 years earlier), but the manner by which Dalton reached his conclusion. Whereas Democritus reached the idea of the existence of atoms through a process of reasoning, Dalton could support his ideas by experimentation. In that difference lay an important landmark in the development of human thought: in matters relating to the physical world empirical (ie experimental) observation had replaced speculative philosophy.

One of the most important early scientific experimenters was the Frenchman Lavoisier, who led Chemistry into modern times with several discoveries about the nature of matter, particularly gases and the air we breathe. The inquisitive spirit with the experimental urge is also evident early in this century in Marie Curie who developed our understanding of radioactivity, and in Alfred Nobel who survived a series of accidents to discover dynamite. Nobel was to become a millionaire and endow the annual prizes named after him.

It only takes a little thought to see the extent to which Chemistry lies behind much of what we take for granted in everyday life today. Our use of oil is illustrative of this. Its heavy compounds are used to make tar for building roads; lighter compounds are used for industrial and domestic fuels as well as for an enormous range of commodities from plastics to pharmaceuticals.

The processes that turn the crude, unrefined liquid that is extracted from the ground into these essentials of modern society are chemical processes. They are the processes that produce the paper of the page you are reading and the ink that printed it. Chemistry lies behind much of modern medicine, food production, sewerage systems, electricity, explosives and plastics.

Chemistry is also about the fundamental nature of matter. Chemistry does not just tell you how soap is made: it will tell you about the chemical reaction – the saponification of animal fats – that lies behind its production. It helps us understand what matter consists of at the subatomic level of electrons, neutrons and protons and how these govern the chemical behaviour of materials. The study of Chemistry opens one's eyes to a whole range of phenomena and theories of matter about which most people are naturally curious.

Subject criteria

AS

Formulae, equations and amounts of substance: atomic mass, simple titrations

Atomic structure: subatomic particles, orbitals

Bonding & structure: states of matter, ionic and covalent bonding, molecular shape

Energetics: concept of enthalpy change in reaction, formation and combustion

Kinetics: collision theory, role of catalysts

Equilibria: dynamic equilibria, factors affecting equilibria

Redox: reduction and oxidation, oxidation state, electron transfer

Inorganic chemistry & the periodic table: Gp II and Gp VII elements, trends in properties across a period

Organic chemistry: functional groups, isomers, classification of reactions

A2

Further energetics: lattice enthalpy, Born-Haber cycle

Further kinetics: determination and use of empirical rate equations of form

Further equilibria: equilibrium constants, Bronsted-Lowry theory of acid-base reactions, dissociation constants

Further redox: simple redox titrations

Further inorganic chemistry: trends in reactions of elements across a period, transition metals

Further organic chemistry: structure of benzene, futher classification of reactions, stereo isomers, organic synthesis and analysis

Modern analytical techniques: spectrometry, NMR

Options

All three major awarding bodies offers A-level Chemistry. OCR offers two specifications, A and B. Specification B refers to Salters Chemistry: a functional approach where chemical principles are presented in the context of applications of chemistry. Salters science specifications are supported by a comprehensive set of student and teacher materials.

The subject criteria determine that A2 builds on AS but some options are available. The following are a sample of those available for optional study in A2:

- Biochemistry
- Environmental Chemistry
- Analysis and detection.

Coursework

All Chemistry specifications require candidates to carry out experimental and investigative activities. These are assessed as either coursework or practical examination or an option of the two. Other coursework options are available on some specifications. The coursework option of the AQA specification is worth 15% of the total marks for AS and 12.5% of the total marks for the A-level.

Course information

Requirements
Normally GCSE Chemistry or Combined Science together with Maths at grades C or above; some institutions may insist on B grades in these subjects.

Goes well with
All maths, science and social science subjects.

Higher education suitability
All science and medically oriented degree courses. May be explicitly or implicitly required for medical, veterinary degrees and those in biological sciences.

Suggested reading
P.W. Atkins. *The Elements of Physical Chemistry*. OUP
A. Atkinson. *Modern Organic Chemistry*. Stanley Thornes
J. Raffan & B. Ratcliff. *Foundation Chemistry*. CUP
B. Ratcliff. *Advanced Practical Chemistry*. CUP

CLASSICAL CIVILISATION

What exactly is the legacy of Greece and Rome? The very question appears to place their impact on our lives at the level of a mere 'influence', but the fact that we can trace back to the achievements of the Athenians and Romans so much of the way we think, create, govern ourselves and live makes it more accurate to say that their two cities are the begetters of western culture, its philosophy, literature, art and political organisation.

Classical Studies is first and foremost a study of specific aspects of Athenian and Roman society, in particular their systems of politics and government (*democracy* is a Greek word), religion and education together with their family life and social conditions. It involves an examination of their moral values, their treatment of slaves and the status they afforded women. It is also an opportunity to learn about their achievements, in particular those that have survived to this day. However, in talking about this period of European history, we must avoid clichés (such as 'The Glory that was Greece and Rome') and learn to draw conclusions from first-hand examination of original evidence, which may be literary, artistic, archaeological or historical. On the Greek side this will include the epic poetry of Homer (the *Odyssey* and the *Iliad*), the tragic drama of Aeschylus, Sophocles and Euripides, the philosophy of Aristotle and Plato and the history written by Herodotus and Thucydides as well as the physical remains of this era (archaeological sites such as those at Athens, Delphi and Olympia). On the Roman side it includes the epic poetry of Vergil (the *Aeneid*), the satires of Horace, Petronius and Juvenal and the historical writings of Caesar, Tacitus and Suetonius as well as Roman buildings and civil architecture.

A study of this evidence leaves us with a clearer sense of the differences not only between Athenian and Roman society but also between both of them and our own. Athenian democracy, for example, throws light on the advantages and disadvantages of our own political system, whilst an analysis of the moral values of ancient societies challenges our modern preconceptions and prejudices.

Though the Romans recognised that they were inferior to the Greeks in artistic creativity and intellectual originality, they saw themselves as their superiors in the art of practical government, and it was this ability to enforce order and sta-bility that made then so formidably effective. In his great patriotic poem, the *Aeneid*, Vergil gave his fellow countrymen a vision of their divine mission to rule the world. The Greeks might surpass them as sculptors, architects and philosophers, but *their* art was 'to impose the rule of law'. The new world order they created was, of course, achieved at a price – the price of liberty – and this is what makes the study of the Roman Empire so perennially relevant. The Romans gave us the word 'liberty', but how much liberty did they enjoy under the emperors? What is more important: liberty, or security?

Subject criteria

The subject criteria require study of the Greek and Roman civilisations in two of the option areas for AS (see below) and three for A-level.

Candidates are further required to:

- study material through primary classical sources

- understand classical values and concepts

- understand, interpret, analyse, evaluate and use a range of evidence from primary classical sources.

Options

Options laid down in the subject criteria:

Architecture: techniques of construction, style and types of buildings

Art: different media, eg sculpture, mosaic; different styles; chronological development

Archaeology: important sites, techniques and the use of evidence

History, politics and society: slavery, city states, economics and agriculture

Literature: different genres from specific authors

Philosophy and values: Stoicism, Epicureanism, religions, concepts of society.

Examples of options within specifications:

- Athenian democracy

- The life and times of Cicero

- Women in Athens and Rome.

Coursework

Coursework requirements vary between specifications. The AQA specification for example requires an essay from a choice of topics for both AS and A2. The coursework component is worth 30% of the total marks for both AS and A-level in this example.

Course information

Requirements

GCSE English at grade C or above is likely to be required, as is History if previously taken.

Goes well with

Most subjects, but some overlap with Ancient History.

Higher education suitability

Most arts subjects, particularly English, modern languages, History, History of Art, Law, Philosophy.

Suggested reading

Recommended texts will depend largely on options to be studied. Some more general examples are as follows.

A. Andrews. *Greek Society*. Penguin

M. Beard & M. Crawford. *Rome in the Late Republic*. Duckworth

J. Boardman et al. *The Oxford History of the Classical World*. OUP

D. Taylor. *Roman Society*. Macmillan

S. Usher. *Historians of Greece & Rome*. Bristol

COMMUNICATION STUDIES

We all communicate or are on the receiving end of 'communication' every day of our lives. We listen to the radio, watch television and videos, read newspapers and magazines, glance at advertising hoardings, perhaps listen to a sermon on Sunday. We also read instruction manuals, job applications, prospectuses, holiday brochures, stop and listen to a sales talk without a moment's thought. In all these cases someone is trying to communicate with us.

It also works the other way round. We may find ourselves in the workplace having to communicate with colleagues, with subordinates and superiors, perhaps also with other parties or organisations such as customers or trade unions. Our daily routine may require us to compose, draw, design, write, take photographs, talk, debate, interpret, use the telephone, appear on television, direct traffic, control aircraft, teach children, teach adults.

The formal study of communication is concerned with the mechanics and theory of communication. How is it done? What makes for effective communication? Is a piece of writing likely to appeal or bore – and why? How are pictures and images exploited by the mass media? What are the motives behind a piece of public communication – are they honourable or cynical? Do soap operas undermine or reinforce social values? Does television convey negative images of black people? Can newspapers ever be unbiased? How far does the 'perception' and the 'context' of the communicator and the receiver affect the way the message is interpreted?

Electronic communication has changed the world in which we live. The student of Communication Studies will consider the impact of the new technologies: the explosion in personal communication facilities through developments such as the mobile phone and the world wide web; the advantages and the disadvantages of email in terms of person to person communication; and the emerging communication cultures on the Internet.

Finally, the student of communication will look at communication issues theoretically. He will learn how values and political beliefs are intertwined with their effective communication. He will explore such matters as political control over public and private communication. He will examine formal theories of communication. He will unravel the assumptions that lie behind the use of the English language which, in accordance with historical precedent, often uses – as in this paragraph – the masculine pronoun to refer to women as well as men.

It's a big and interesting subject. Has this page communicated anything about it?

Subject criteria

There are no subject criteria for Communication Studies at A-level. The following unit titles are available for study.

AS

Introducing communication practice: Processes and strategies of communication theory

Text & meanings in communication: The construction of meaning in communications texts

Themes in personal communication: Verbal, non-verbal, intra-personal and group communication

A2

Developing communications practice: Project on the production of a communications artefact from brief through to evaluation

Culture, context & communication: Role in organisational, local, national and global contexts

Issues in communication: Current debates and controversies

Coursework

AS Communication Studies requires the production of a portfolio including a 500-word essay on research together with a presentation. A2 coursework entails the project detailed above. Coursework contributes 40% of the marks in both AS and A-level.

Course information

Requirements
GCSE English at grade C or above is likely to be required.

Goes well with
English, Sociology, Psychology, Art, photography, History of Art.

Higher education suitability
Any arts, social science or vocational subject; useful for anyone planning a career in film, advertising, journalism, television, teaching, or those wishing to study business or social sciences.

Suggested reading

R. Dimbleby & G. Burton. *More Than Words*. Routledge
G. Dyer. *Advertising as Communication*. Routledge
J. Fiske. *Introduction to Communication Studies*. Routledge
J. Hartley. *Understanding News*. Routledge

COMPUTING

People have used devices to speed up calculations for many centuries, but the first 'electronic computer' in the modern sense was built in America during the Second World War. It was 100 feet long, and had 17,000 vacuum tubes ('valves'), 40 instrument panels and 6,000 switches. Today a personal computer, tens of thousands of times more powerful and small enough to hold in the palm of your hand, can be purchased for less than £1,000.

The world wide web has brought an unparalleled wealth of information to millions and allows rapid, cheap communication all over the world. Electronic commerce (e-commerce) and electronic learning (e-learning) are in their infancy but will become the norm within the lifetime of this book. The rate of change is staggering. The millions of pounds spent globally to combat the largely fictitious millennium bug give an indication of our reliance on computer systems worldwide

Most aspects of computing fall into one of four categories: theory, hardware, software and applications.

Computing theory begins by defining a special type of machine whose behaviour can be rigidly defined and determined. This is the basic model of a computer. Almost all computers are 'digital', which means that they recognise data and instructions only in the form of zeros and ones. Computing theory studies how this apparently inadequate 'language' can be used to express numbers, letters, shapes and more complex ideas like 'a holiday for two in Tenerife'. It also examines the logical processes by which real-life problems can be solved by computers: how to get them to add up a series of numbers or sort a list of names into alphabetical order.

Computer hardware is that part of the system that may be seen or touched and consists of four main parts: an input device (most commonly a keyboard); a processor (the part that processes inputted data according to a set of instructions or the 'program'); a memory device and finally an output device such as a screen or printer.

Computer software is a term referring to the instructions that control the behaviour of the hardware, the processing of information fed into the computer and the manner of its presentation.

Computer applications: computers exist to perform tasks (financial, clerical, mechanical) and to solve problems efficiently and usually more speedily than humans. The study of computer applications involves on the one hand a study of systems analysis (in which activities, tasks, or organisations to be 'computerised' are analysed so that the correct hardware and software can be provided), and on the other a broader study of how computers affect society as a whole.

Subject criteria

Both AS and A-level are required to address the following topics. The requirement for AS to cover every item of the criteria is less than that of A-level provided a balance is maintained.

Applications & Effects: Purpose and impact of computing applications, information system, user interface, systems development life cycle, consequences of current use of computing

Hardware & Communications: Processors, input, output and storage devices, connection between devices, characteristics of networks, future developments

Software: Systems software, software packages, data types and structures, programming paradigms, problem solving

Information: Status, source, ownership, currency and accuracy, organisation and structuring, methods of finding, selecting and managing information

Options
Examples of available units include:

- Design & organisation of information systems

- Computer systems design

- Computer systems, programming & networking concepts

- Principles of hardware, software & applications.

Coursework
The subject criteria require a minimum of 16.7% of the total work as the coursework component. The Edexcel specification for example includes two projects: an AS project on System Design & Development and an A2 project on Software design & development. In this example coursework contributes 33.3% of the total marks in both AS and A-level.

Course information

Requirements
Keen interest in computers, though not necessarily extensive experience; English Language and Maths GCSE desirable.

Goes well with
Any subject.

Higher education suitability
Most degree courses; not necessary for Computer Science degrees.

Suggested reading
R. Bradley. *Understanding Computer Science for A Level*. Stanley Thornes
P.M. Heathcote. *Advanced Level Computing*. Letts
R. White. *How Computers Work*. QUE

DESIGN & TECHNOLOGY

Design is the creative process behind much of our material environment.
It is a broad field of endeavour, ranging from decoration at one end of the
spectrum to heavy engineering at the other. Yoked to Art, it tends towards
the decorative arts. Combined with technology, it deals with our practical and
industrial needs.

The servant of technological design is craft. Craftsmen use skills that to a
large extent have been handed down to them: their work tends to be
evolutionary rather than revolutionary in character. Designers, by contrast,
have to develop innovative solutions to problems, via lateral thought
processes. Industrial designers are not independent artists, following their
own creative inspiration; they must be sensitive to consumer demand and to
the situation on the shop-floor. It is not enough for their products to look
beautiful; they must ensure that the manufacturer has the materials, tools
and understanding to translate their designs into reality.

The pioneer of modern industrial design was Raymond Loewy, a Frenchman
who made his career in the US after 1919. He hit on the idea that you could
attract passengers to railway travel by streamlining trains to look like sleek,
futuristic aircraft. He went on to change the face of America: Greyhound
buses, Lucky Strike packets, refrigerators, toasters, all bore his mark. He is
perhaps the best example of the industrial designer as artist and image-maker.
After Loewy, design became a fundamental part of marketing.

Modern industrial design is a complex process that has to take account of
rapid change. Computer-driven tools have led to shorter production runs.
The miniaturisation of mechanisms has brought about a marked reduction in
the scale of products. New composites have made it possible to produce
lightweight goods. Contemporary designers have a wide range of options;
but must also be aware, as never before, of their environmental
responsibilities. In the age of recycling, we are likely to move towards
'design for disassembly'.

There are many reasons why Design & Technology should take its place in
the mainstream of education. The design process is an education in itself.
Designers deliver the best outcome from the resources available. That means
devising a range of possible solutions to be tested, justified, modified. The
approach is creative and highly motivating. Design students learn through
practical experience to be analytical, methodical and self-critical – skills and
habits of thought that are useful in all walks of life. Design & Technology
also holds the key to the future success of the British economy, equipping us
to make a positive contribution to society.

Subject criteria

Skills, knowledge and understanding are not differentiated between AS and A-level within the subject criteria.

For AS-level the above should be set in the context of:

* materials, components and their uses

* industrial and commercial practices

* product development.

A-level specifications are additionally required to include:

* an in-depth study related to the focus area (see *Options* below)

* a designing and making activity.

Below is a summary of skills and knowledge as required by both qualifications.

Designing: Developing design briefs and proposals, use of a systems approach, use of ICT for designing, modelling and communicating

Planning: Equipment and process selection, time and resources management, use of ICT for planning and data handling

Evaluating: Degree of accuracy required

Making: Working with materials, components and appropriate technologies, planning optimum use of materials, use of performance testing of products

Materials & components: Principles and techniques of testing, working characteristics of materials

Industrial & commercial practice: Main features of manufacturing industry, stages of production, customer service

Quality: In terms of the product and the human process of designing and making

Health & Safety: Legislative framework, risk assessment, safe working practice

Systems & control: Production, quality assurance, resources and people, design of control systems

Products & applications: Manufacturing processes, social, political and ethical influences on design, production and sale

Options
Design & Technology is offered in three *focus areas*:

- Product design

- Food

- Systems & control.

All the subject criteria above apply in each case.

Coursework
The subject criteria require that a minimum of 30% of the total marks should be internally assessed. In the AQA specification for example, coursework in AS comprises project and/or portfolio work on aspects of industrial and commercial practice. This is augmented by a project for A-level students combining designing and making skills. Coursework for AS in this example forms 30% of total marks and 35% for A-level.

Course information

Requirements
A problem-solving approach; research and analytical skills and good commuication skills; imagination and an 'eye' for design.

Goes well with
Any subject.

Higher education suitability
Most useful for Engineering degree courses; a useful third A-level for a wide range of other degree subjects.

Suggested reading
J. Morrison & J. Twyford. *Design Capability & Awareness*. Longman
Peter Dormer. *Design Since 1945*. Thames & Hudson

DRAMA & THEATRE STUDIES

Theatre, as an art form and a ritualisation of human utterance and action, dates back to our prehistory. Theatrical activity is as old as the formation of men and women into social groups; and by as early a period as the 5th century BC the Greeks had developed theatre into high art – some would say to a pitch not matched since, and indeed they built theatres and wrote plays that still influence us today. Nor was this just a Western ritual: theatre also flourished from earliest times in Japan, China and Africa.

A study of theatre is also a study of the component parts of a theatrical production, most notably the text. Most theatrical texts are published and in that form are traditionally the concern of the student of English Literature; but while nearly all dramatic texts have claims to be regarded as literature, they are first and foremost the basis of a theatrical performance and should really be viewed as such. A study of texts seeks to answer questions such as 'What makes a text dramatic?' and 'What works on the stage, and why?'

Texts may also be viewed from the perspective of the dramatists who write them; and any study of theatre involves an historical study of the major playwrights of the world, from Aristophanes to Samuel Beckett.

Further, a dramatic text is an art form which needs interpretation. Just as music needs a conductor, a play needs a director and actors. The study of theatre involves examining theories of interpretation and significant interpreters in theatrical history. Until the 20th century, it was the actors and actresses who alone caught the public imagination and engaged our interest; in recent years audiences have become more conscious of the director.

A dramatic production is an enterprise which depends for its effects on more than just a text and some directed actors. It requires the support of a wide range of technical skills, including those involving costumes, design, lighting, sound and a host of other artifices.

Finally, drama must be seen in its social context, both historically and contemporarily. Regarded by some (not correctly) as purely entertainment, the theatre has, nevertheless, always been more than merely a medium to make us laugh or cry. Respected for its unique power to release private and public feeling, and feared on account of its potential influence on public opinion (an influence that is often out of all proportion to its immediate audience), drama has frequently been the victim of political censorship. Theatre can touch a raw public nerve.

Subject criteria

There are no QCA subject criteria for Drama & Theatre Studies. AQA, Edexcel and WJEC offer specifications in this subject. The course content outlined below is from the Edexcel specification.

Course content

AS

Exploration of Drama & Theatre: Coursework study of two plays from the point of view of performers, designers and directors

Text in performance I: Students undertake a role in the production of a play; externally examined by visiting examiner

Text in Context I: Students demonstrate their understanding of the play in the unit described above and also that of a further live theatre production

A2

Devising: Group project on devising an original piece of drama; students are internally assessed on their individual performance

Text in performance II: An in-depth study of one further play; students demonstrate the essence of their interpretation in a workshop assessed by a visiting examiner

Text in context II: One play from a choice of two studied from the point of view of a director; study and research the production of a play performed between 1575 and 1720

Options

The Edexcel specification offers suggestions for plays to be studied rather than listing options. An exception to this rule is Unit 6, which requires the study of *The Trojan Woman* by Euripides or the *Beggar's Opera* by John Gay for candidates taking their A-level in 2002 or 2003. In the AQA AS coursework unit one skill is nominated for assessment taken from Acting, Costume design & construction, Mask design & construction, Design & execution of stage settings and lighting and/or sound. Plays studied for other units of the specification are chosen from a number of themes and periods, eg The twentieth century & contemporary drama.

Coursework

In the Edexcel specification, Unit 1 (AS) and Unit 4 (A2) as described above are assessed by coursework that contributes 30% of marks to the AS award and 35% of the A-level. The AQA specification also has an AS unit: Devised drama and an A2 unit: Practical – play in production assessed by coursework. Here coursework is 40% of both the AS and A-level total marks.

Course information

Requirements
GCSE English at grade C or above is likely to be required.

Goes well with
Any arts subject.

Higher education suitability
Good preparation for a range of degree courses in the arts and humanities; because of its academic content this A-level may count towards matriculation, but admissions tutors for subjects outside the arts and humanities may not regard the subject as meeting their course requirements.

Suggested reading
M. Banham. *The Cambridge Guide to Theatre*. CUP
E. Bentley. *The Theory of the Modern Stage*. Penguin
P. Hartnoll. *A Concise History of the Theatre*. Thames & Hudson
S. Mackey. *Practical Theatre: A Post-16 Approach*. Stanley Thornes

ECONOMICS

Economics has been defined as the practical science of the production and distribution of wealth. The resources from which we create our wealth – natural ones such as oil and human ones such as labour – are limited and hotly fought over. It is the economist who studies this competition and how we make use of these limited resources in order to meet our needs (whether they be for food, housing, video-recorders or foreign holidays).

Microeconomics

With a personal allowance of £25 a week, do you spend it on your addiction to chocolate, on a ticket to an away football match, or do you save it? £25 doesn't cover all these plans and your limited resources force you to choose between alternatives. Economists seek to explain how we make these choices and what their consequences are. This branch of the subject is known as 'Household Behaviour'.

Businesses face similar issues. Should a company encourage overtime among its workforce or should it recruit extra staff – or should it buy a new and more efficient machine? Economists describe this branch of the subject as the 'Theory of the Firm'.

Household Behaviour and the Theory of the Firm form part of what is known as 'Microeconomics', that part of the subject that deals with individual elements of the economy.

Macroeconomics

Macroeconomics is the study of the whole economy and of how the different parts interact. It deals with questions such as what determines the level of exports and imports and why some countries have slower economic growth than others. An important part of macroeconomics is the focus on government policy. Would lower interest rates lead to lower employment or will lower taxes cause higher inflation? Clearly these questions have political as well as economic implications: the study of Economics is the study of the world we live in and its attendant problems of unemployment, poverty, and environmental damage.

Economics gives us the framework for making sense of the world of trade. It does this by establishing simplifying assumptions that make this world easier to understand (economic theory). For example, an important part of Economics is the study of supply and demand. In practice, all forces that affect supply and demand are constantly changing and this makes cause and effect hard to identify. In the first instance, economists try to examine what would happen if only one variable, perhaps consumer incomes, were to change. From this starting point they go on to modify their simplifying assumptions and apply their analysis to the real world – which is what is meant by 'Applied Economics'.

Subject criteria

As in many other specifications the requirements differentiating AS from A-level involve depth of study as opposed to what is studied. AS level requires the use of basic models to explore current economic behaviour whilst A-level requires more complex modelling and wider application.

Economic choices & markets

Reasons for choices by individuals, organisations and societies

How competitive markets work

Competition and competitive behaviour

Why markets may not work efficiently

Impact of government intervention on markets

The national & international economy

Government policy objectives and national performance indicators

Aggregate demand and aggregate supply: Output, employment and prices

Application of macroeconomic policy instruments

International transactions

Options

Examples of unit titles available include:

- The national & international economy

- Economics of work & leisure

- Transport economics

- Working as an economist

- Business economics & the distribution of income.

Coursework

Economics specifications may or may not contain a coursework element. Coursework is optional in the AQA A-level specification, consists of a 4000-word investigation of any area of economics and is worth 20% of the total marks.

Course information

Requirements

GCSE Maths and English at grades C or above are likely to be required.

Goes well with
Any subject.

Higher education suitability
A wide range of social science degree courses; not necessary for Economics degrees, though helpful in the first year.

Suggested reading
A. Anderton. *Economics*. Causeway Press
J. Beardshaw et al. *Economics: A Students' Guide*. Pitman
G. Stanlake & S. Grant. *Introductory Economics*. Longmans

ENGLISH LANGUAGE

Most of us learned English when we were small and we probably now speak it fluently. We will have been taught how to spell, write grammatical sentences, recognise a piece by Shakespeare for what it is, enjoy a good debate, know that a note to the bank manager is not the same as a love letter or a piece of journalism describing river pollution. We may write poetry. We may also know something about English in other parts of the world – that, for instance, in America they say 'fall' instead of 'autumn' and spell differently, and that even in this country there are regional variations in syntax and accent. We are able to communicate freely using written and spoken English for a wide variety of purposes; we have probably passed English GCSE.

So what more is there to learn? Maybe not much, except that most of us only know how to do these things intuitively. By studying our language we can render intuitions explicit and 'realise' what we already know.

An understanding of the different contemporary examples of English leads to a better awareness of the different uses to which language may be put and the different forms those uses require. We use English above all to communicate a message: an invitation to tea, a test-match commentary, a booklet explaining how to work a video recorder, a set of military standing orders. We use English to influence people: a vicar's sermon, a politician's rhetoric. We use English to entertain: a pop song, a story, a piece of theatre.

A study of English is in large part a study of its uses and of the character of the language associated with those uses. What is it that makes the journalism of the *Sun* newspaper so different from that of *The Times* or *Daily Telegraph*?

Reflections on English language give rise to a wide range of language issues. Is it wrong to say 'hopefully' in the way that many people do, 'wrongly', today? Why is there such a thing as so-called 'grammatical' English? Does it matter if we allow American usage to creep into the language spoken in this country? Periodically there is a debate about whether we should reform the way we spell words (consider how we say 'cough', 'enough', 'plough'). To do so would remove some of the barriers to learning how to read and write. Why are we resistant to such a move? How does one counter the argument that keeping English difficult bolsters the power and status of those who 'can' against those who 'can't'? English is also a political issue.

Subject criteria

AS

Frameworks for the systematic study of the English language:

- characteristic speech sounds and intonation patterns
- the vocabulary of English
- grammar, the forms and structures of words, sentences and texts
- semantics and pragmatics, construction and interpretation of meanings in speech and writing
- variations in language according to mode and context

A2

A deeper knowledge and understanding of frameworks as in *AS* above

Application and usefulness of different frameworks for the description and analysis of speech and writing

Analysis and evaluation of historical and geographical variation in the meanings and form of language

The use and evaluation of knowledge and understanding as tools for the analysis of language in use

Common to AS & A2

- application of linguistic concepts and frameworks
- variation in spoken and written language
- control of spoken and written English for a variety of audiences or purposes
- comment on the production, interpretation, adaptation and representation of texts

Options

Unit titles include:

- Description of English
- Variation and development in English
- Language contexts, social & structural
- Varieties of English
- The language of the media.

Coursework

May be optional on AS. Coursework forms 30% of total marks for both AS and A-level on the OCR specification and either 15% or 30% for A-level in the Edexcel version depending on options.

Course information

Requirements

A minimum of GCSE English at grade C or above; grade B may be required by some institutions.

Goes well with

Any arts A-level, particularly a classical or modern language.

Higher education suitability

Excellent preparation for arts-based degree courses.

Suggested reading

D. Freeborn. *From Old English to Standard English.* Macmillan
A. Goddard et al. *English Language A Level: The Starter Pack.* Framework Press
C. McDonald. *English Language Project Work.* Macmillan
S. Thorne. *Mastering Advanced English Language.* Macmillan

ENGLISH LITERATURE

Drama may claim to be the oldest genre of English Literature, though it may be wondered why we call it literature and not just drama. The fact is that the 'scripts' of dramatic productions (preserved orally or in written form) meet many of the criteria of literature; further, they are often in verse.

Poetry, or more accurately, **verse**, may well claim to be as old as drama since, as has been pointed out, drama was often written in verse form. Verse may be distinguished from prose by the two characteristics it almost invariably possesses: an identifiable rhythm or metre (more or less, but not entirely, regular) and a white space at the end of each line – since most verse follows rules that limit the number of sounds or syllables in any one line. Verse also has other characteristics, such as a preponderance of literary or poetic devices, for example metaphor and rhyme, though these are also to be found in much prose writing.

The **novel**, as its title implies, is a relatively new genre in English (and European) literature. There was little tradition of stories in prose (they were harder to remember) until the development of faster and more economic printing. Other factors, as much economic and political as literary, conspired with these industrial developments to bring about a form of literature that was written to be read in private rather than to be spoken aloud or declaimed from the stage. Not least of these was the growth of middle-class leisure (novels take a long time to read), the changes in architecture that provided for private rooms in large houses (novels need peace and quiet) as well as the emergence of middle-class values that found their best literary expression not in subversive drama or flowery poetry but in the prosaic form of the novel, which sounded a new note of realism. The individualism that lay at the heart of these values and that emerged at the start of the 18th century was given vivid literary expression by Daniel Defoe in *Robinson Crusoe*. Defoe was followed in a different vein but similar spirit by Fielding and Richardson, and the tradition of the novel was firmly established.

Why do we study literature? Most people would probably reply 'for pleasure'. Studying a classic or difficult book can often give more lasting pleasure than an easy one, the mark of a classic being that it yields an inexhaustible wealth of fresh insights at every reading. Young children read in order to escape into a world of the imagination – an escapism that in later years becomes more positive as literature allows us to widen our emotional sympathies, to see the world from many different angles, to 'be' other people rather than remaining confined to one limited self. More importantly, literature is about values. As we read we are forced to take sides and to pass moral judgement. We compare our reactions with those of others in order to defend our opinions or to modify them in the light of argument. Quite uniquely, literature takes the most important issues of our lives and presents them through a carefully contrived representation of supposedly real or deliberately idealised life.

Subject criteria

AS

Show knowledge & understanding of:

- a minimum of four texts covering prose, poetry and drama; includes a Shakespeare play and one other text pre-1900
- how texts relate to the contexts in which they were written
- different ways of interpretation of texts by different readers

Should be able to:

- read, analyse and communicate accurately and effectively
- understand and evaluate how writers use form, structure and language
- produce fluent and convincing responses
- draw upon understanding of different interpretations
- make appropriate use of critical concepts and terminology

A2

Show knowledge & understanding of:

- a minimum of four further texts covering prose, poetry and drama; at least one work published before 1770 and one before 1900
- the importance of cultural and historical influences and the relevance of the author's life
- the significance of literary traditions, periods and movements
- the ways in which texts are interpreted and valued by different people in different times

Should be able to:

- comment on differences and commonality between substantial whole texts
- synthesise their knowledge and understanding of styles, contents and meanings

Options

A choice of texts is available in all specifications, some examples are given at the end of this section. Specifications differ in their requirements for examination with or without open texts. Coursework units may be optional on particular areas of the specification.

Coursework

Coursework is optional for both AS and A-level in the Edexcel specification where it accounts for 15% of the total marks in each case. The AS coursework option is available for the Shakespeare component and the A2 for modern prose. Alternatively in the OCR specification coursework is available in AS as a compulsory literature complementary study concerning a text of the candidate's choice and comprising 30% of total marks. As part of A2 coursework is optional for the post-1914 prose component and together with the AS coursework is worth 30% of the total marks for A-level.

Course information

Requirements
GCSE English at grade C or above will almost certainly be required; candidates who have taken English Literature GCSE will also be required to offer a minimum of grade C.

Goes well with
Arts and social sciences.

Higher education suitability
Wide range of degree courses in the humanities, including English, American Studies, European Studies, Philosophy.

Sample texts

Prose
V. Brittain. *Testament of Youth.* Virago
L. De Bernieres. *Captain Corelli's Mandolin.* Vintage
T. Hardy. *The Return of the Native*
M. Shelley. *Frankenstein*
J. Austen. *Emma*
C. Dickens. *Hard Times*

Poetry
E. Jennings. *Selected Poems.* Carcanet
J. Betjeman. *Best of Betjeman.* Penguin
J. Keats. *Selected Poems.* Everyman
Penguin Book of American Verse
S.T. Coleridge. *Selected Poems.* Everyman

Drama

A. Behn. *The Rover.* New Mermaids
B. Friel. *Translations.* Faber
C. Churchill. *Top Girls.* Methuen
T. Williams. *A Streetcar Named Desire.* Penguin
B. Shaw. *The Devil's Disciple.* Penguin
W. Shakespeare. *Henry V*
 Antony & Cleopatra
 The Winter's Tale
 Much Ado About Nothing
 Hamlet

ENVIRONMENTAL SCIENCE

Aerosols and the ozone layer; passive smoking and lung cancer; paper wastage and the destruction of the rainforest; leaking supertankers and polluted beaches; genetically modified organisms and organic food production: these are the issues that capture our attention today, focusing concern on the environment and our treatment of it to a degree that would have been inconceivable 20 years ago. The effect of technologically advanced societies on our planet is no longer just the concern of cranky political groups. Since space satellites have sent back hard evidence of mankind's devastating impact on our surroundings, it is now not only acceptable to be 'green': to be so is to address one of society's most urgent problems.

A study of these issues has two stages. First, it involves an examination of the facts about the world we live in and the impact of our behaviour on it. This requires investigations into areas of study that we normally see as quite separate from each other. Thus a study of the earth and its life systems involves a study of Biology (plant and animal life), Geology (rocks and minerals), Chemistry (the composition of the natural and manufactured world), Physics (the forces operating within the earth and its atmosphere) and finally Geography (the physical world, its land forms, oceans and weather, together with the two-way relationship between these phenomena and mankind). Just as men and women are constrained by the physical world they inhabit, so the delicate balances on which that world depends are increasingly liable to serious interference by their unbridled behaviour. A study of these phenomena – a true interdisciplinary exercise – is the stuff and substance of Environmental Science.

However, facts give rise to wider considerations, as we increase our awareness of environmental issues. The pressures that lead to many of the excesses of human behaviour (as when we seek to provide and use scarce resources in order to fulfil our needs – such as those for fossil fuels) – are explained by Economics. They may also be see in terms of Government and Politics (as when the government sought to avoid siting the Channel rail link too close to its supporters' back gardens) and Sociology (as the impact on South American Indians, displaced by the destroyers of the rainforests, can testify). The perspectives of all these academic disciplines must at times be brought to bear on environmental issues. Environmental Science examines the cumulative impact of individually unrelated events; it places scientific evidence in a perspective that we ignore at our peril.

There are no subject criteria for Environmental Science. The subject is offered by a single examining board, the AQA.

Specification content

AS

Energy, the atmosphere & the hydrosphere: Energy transfer, human needs for energy and water, the 'greenhouse' effect, global climate change

The lithosphere: Components of the earth's crust, effect of overexploitation, sustainable management, environmental impact, strategies for enhancing the environment

The Biosphere: Essential life processes, energy capture, use and transfer, productivity and dynamics of ecosystems, population dynamics, effect of human population growth, need for biodiversity, strategies for conservation

A2

Biotic resource management: Management of biotic resources to satisfy the demands of human populations (terminal component drawing on AS study, to be taken at the end of the course)

Pollution & physical resource management: A global perspective on sustainable development through management of resources; pollution, recycling, reuse (terminal component drawing on AS study, to be taken at the end of the course)

Either

Practical investigation

Candidates choice of subject demonstrating ability to:

- plan and design experiment
- present data in graphical form
- analyse data using appropriate statistical treatment
- interpret and evaluate experimental data

(terminal component drawing on AS study, to be taken at the end of the course)

Or

Written unit testing similar skills as the practical component

Options

Practical skills assessed by investigation or through a written unit as described above.

Coursework

Optional practical unit.

Course information

Requirements

Grade C or above in Combined Science, any of the single sciences and/or Geography would be an advantage.

Goes well with

Any science subject but avoid combining with Biology *and* Geography as the degree of overlap may be perceived as excessive by some providers of higher education.

Higher education suitability

Most degree courses other than Environmental Science/Studies, for which admission tutors prefer Biology, Geography, Chemistry, Physics or Economics A-levels, since the A-level syllabus forms the substance of much of the first year of any degree course.

Suggested reading

D, Drew. *Man – Environment Processes.* George Allen & Unwin
I. Simmons. *Biogeographical Processes.* George Allen & Unwin

FILM STUDIES

Film Studies is a multi-disciplinary subject, crossing the boundaries of Photography, Sociology, History, Literature and Art. Film has done more than any other art to reflect and shape the cultural and moral climate of the 20th century. No other art has evolved so rapidly, or reached such a vast international public.

The years during and after the First World War witnessed an explosion of film as an art form and as big business. The major artistic genius of this era, D.W. Griffith, was a technical innovator, but he was interested above all in using the camera to create a new kind of drama – which in turn demanded a new kind of acting. The fact that this cinema was wordless gave it an international passport, and made it possible for Charlie Chaplin, the other genius of this era, to turn film comedy into a universal language.

While competing Hollywood studios were giving the American public what it wanted, the film industries of Europe were developing in other directions. Al Jolson's *The Jazz Singer* (1927) was, famously, the first 'talkie', but it was the invention of 'Movietone' in 1931 that really ushered in the new age of sound. The screenwriter suddenly became as important to a film's success as the director, the camera crew and the stars. The 1930s were the years when Hollywood developed its classic genres – the musical, the western, the gangster movie, the thriller – each with its own conventions and clichés. At the end of the decade came colour, used to spectacular effect in *Gone With the Wind* (1939) which remained the biggest box office smash hit for half a century after its production.

Like Soviet Russia, Nazi Germany was not slow to exploit the cinema for the purposes of propaganda, for instance in Leni Riefenstahl's film of the Berlin Olympic Games of 1938 – a glorification of the 'new' Germany.

During the Second World War cinema audiences broke new records as films helped to keep up morale. The cinema created, or reinforced, social solidarity far more effectively than official propaganda. But by the late 1950s the commercial cinema, faced with the challenge of television, was changing radically. British films turned away from the cheerful stereotypes of the Ealing comedies to the social realism of *Saturday Night and Sunday Morning* and its successors. From the 1960s onwards, Hollywood producers and directors pushed back the frontiers of taste, or went all out for special effects. Yet some of the most successful directors of this new age, artists such as Francis Ford Coppola, Stanley Kubrick and Steven Spielberg, drew their inspiration from the great tradition.

Cinema is an art, and it is a business. The fascination of Film Studies is the opportunity it affords to explore this continuing contradiction. Or is it a contradiction?

A single awarding body, WJEC, offers Film Studies. There are no QCA subject criteria; the table below outlines the content of the specification.

AS

How a film communicates meaning and engages audiences

How cinema functions as a business

Develop a critical understanding of audience participation as consumers, critics and fans

Identifying messages and values in films, special reference to British/Irish cinema

Practical application of learning, applying knowledge and understanding gained from textual study in practical work such as storyboarding and screenwriting

A2

Further knowledge and understanding of film text and spectatorship, films with common *authorship*, different historical period and cinematic tradition

Further knowledge and appreciation of producers and audiences, locating specific cinema institutions within their economic, social and cultural contexts

Application of critical approaches to the study of film extracts, complete films and groups of films

Application of learning, knowledge and understanding gained from textual and critical study in creative work such as film journalism, screenwriting and video production

Units of assessment

AS

FS1	Film – making meaning 1
FS2	Producers & audiences
FS3	Messages & values – British & Irish cinema

A2

FS4	Film – making meaning 2
FS5	Studies in world cinema
FS6	Critical studies

Coursework

Units FS1 and FS4 contribute 40% of the marks to both AS and A-level. Candidates complete a course portfolio comprising two written analyses featuring specific film sequences and creative work in the development of an imaginary film sequence.

Course information

Requirements

GCSE English at grade C or above is a likely requirement.

Goes well with

Any arts subject other than Media Studies.

Higher education suitability

Most courses related to communications and modern studies.

Suggested reading

D. Cook. *A History of Narrative Film.* W.W. Norton
D. Bordwell & K Thompson. *Film Art: An Introduction.* McGraw Hill

GENERAL STUDIES

General Studies is not a subject in the same sense as History, Physics or Law. In practice the content of a programme of General Studies will reflect the experience, skills and interests of a school's staff and, it is to be hoped, those of their students. In all cases, however, the underlying intention is to ensure that sixth-formers gain a wider perspective on the world than would be the case had they confined themselves to their A-level syllabuses; and also that they increase the range of skills in which they are proficient.

The subject matter is without boundary. It may include, by way of example, any of the following: Music, literary appreciation, comparative literature, poetry, drama, Communication and Media Studies, creative writing, a modern language, contemporary political affairs, studies of the developing world, Economics, Mathematics, Computing, science subjects, Psychology, history of science, Philosophy, word-processing. This is in no sense an exhaustive list.

This type of study not only increases students' knowledge and understanding, thereby broadening their general perspective; the learning of any new subject will develop important skills that have a general usefulness outside the confines of the subject – whether social, intellectual or practical.

Learning a modern language, for instance, develops our attention to detail and teaches us about rules – their purpose as well as their limitations; it also affords a view of the life and history of another country and its background; and it can give us self-confidence. Philosophy teaches us how to apply our reason to issues: it affects the way we think about everything, about the nature of right and wrong, truth itself; it teaches us how to present abstract ideas (usually in written form) in a manner that is coherent and directed, organising diverse evidence into a structured argument. These skills, also developed by the study of many other subjects, are some of the most important we can learn in the sixth form and in higher education.

Just as there are no rules about what may be taught under the heading of General Studies, so there are none about how they may be taught. They may take the form of an additional single field of study, pursued in some depth; or of several, either taken together or in a series of short courses. Teaching or learning may involve traditional talk and chalk, discussions, workshop sessions, debates, video sessions, outside visits and, of course, project work: research, surveys, interviews and the production of student magazines.

Subject criteria

There are no separate subject criteria for AS and A-level General Studies. A-level extends beyond AS in breadth, depth and higher level skills.

Science, maths & technology:

- physical, life and earth sciences
- scientific objectivity
- scientific methods, principles and criteria
- moral responsibility
- mathematical reasoning
- relationship between technology, science, culture and ideology

Culture, morality, arts & humanities:

- beliefs, values and moral reasoning
- religious belief and experience
- the nature and importance of culture
- creativity and innovation
- aesthetic evaluation
- media and communication

Society, politics & the economy:

- ideologies and values in society
- political processes and goals
- explanation and evaluation of human behaviour
- law, culture and ethics
- social and economic trends and constraints

Options

AQA offers two alternative specifications for General Studies (A and B). Coursework is optional in both the AQA and the OCR specifications.

Coursework

In the OCR specification coursework is offered as units in The scientific domain available for AS, and in The social domain in A2. Coursework is worth 30% of the marks in AS and 15–30% in A-level depending on whether both coursework options are taken up. Coursework assignments are set and marked by OCR. AQA coursework is only available as part of A2 and comprises a problem-solving exercise worth 15% of the total marks.

Course information

Requirements
Often no specific GCSEs will be required for General Studies but grades C or above in Maths, English and Science will enhance candidates' chances of success; in many institutions General Studies is a compulsory or expected component of all A-level programmes.

Goes well with
Any subject.

Higher education suitability
Not accepted by most universities either for the purposes of course requirements or as an approved subject for matriculation; General Studies should be taken alongside a full complement of other A-levels – never as an alternative to one of them.

Suggested reading
Newspapers such as the *Guardian* and journals such as *The Economist* constitute a key resource.

P. Higginson. *General Studies Resource Books.* Longman
M. Kirby. *General Studies: A Complete Course & Teacher's Guide.* Pearson

GEOGRAPHY

Geography is a study of the surface features of our planet on the one hand and of the men and women who populate it on the other. It is also a study of the interrelationship between these two phenomena. Geographers today are principally preoccupied with this interrelationship, with the way the physical environment affects us and we affect the physical environment in an ever changing, two-way process. If the Green Party is concerned with the politics of mankind and the environment, it is geographers who describe their interdependent relationship and who are best placed to foresee and help us to avoid catastrophe.

However, in order to understand the way people and the environment interact they must first be understood separately.

Physical Geography involves the study of the earth's surface and of the processes that created it; of the mountains and valleys formed by tectonic movement and retreating glaciers; of the rocks that form these mountains (Geology) and the soil they support (Pedology); of the rivers that flow through them together with the water cycle of which they are a part; and of the coasts that surround them. It also examines the weather that both shapes these physical features and is determined by them (Climatology). Physical geographers ask questions such as: 'What human activities may be contributing to the death of fish in Norwegian fjords?' and 'What effect do skiers have on topsoil and agriculture in the Alps?'

Human Geography looks at populations. Human geographers examine population size and growth (Demography). They study our agriculture, our industry, our transport systems, the environment we create for ourselves in villages, towns, cities and urban sprawls and the various forces – social, economic and political – that affect these matters. Human geographers are fond of explaining our behaviour. They might, for instance, observe that we tend to live close to where we work (or near a motorway that leads directly to our workplace); that we buy milk from the village shop or local supermarket and our car from the nearest town or city; that the number of pubs in a locality is a function of the number of adult males the area supports.

Systematic or **Regional Geography** synthesises the human and physical with reference to a specific area or region such as a town, country or continent. This allows a full exploration of the interrelationships and changes that occur over time. It is specialised work involving knowledge of political, cultural and social aspects of a country as well as physical and human studies. Regional Geography further involves the application of concepts and what are known as 'models' in order to seek and understand patterns in the real world. Through this approach geographers seek to understand changes such as, in the UK, the decline of inner city areas, the different rates of industrial growth, the depopulation of the large conurbations and the increase in population in East Anglia, the South West and the Welsh borders.

Subject criteria

Both AS and A-level criteria require the study of physical, human and environmental geography and also require investigative work including an element of fieldwork. As in many specifications, A-level study requires an increased depth of understanding of processes, concepts, etc.

AS

A range of themes, places and environments to include the United Kingdom and countries in various states of development

Interaction between people and their environment

Selected physical processes: their interactions and outcomes over space and time

Selected human processes: their interactions and outcomes over space and time

A2

A range of themes, places and environments on all scales from local to global in different parts of the world and in different environments to include the United Kingdom and countries in various states of development

Interaction between people and their environment focusing on relevant human and physical systems

Physical processes (terrestrial, atmospheric and biotic): their interactions and outcomes over space and time

Human processes (economic, social, political and cultural): their interactions and outcomes over space and time

Recent ideas, methods and approaches

Synthesis of geographical information in various forms from various sources

AS & A2

Knowledge of:

- geographical terminology, concepts and theories

- location and characteristics of places studied

- processes responsible for the characteristics of places and environments

- interaction of people and their environments

Understanding of:

- significance of spatial and temporal scales
- the role of values and attitudes in geographical issues
- the potential and limitations of evidence, approaches, concepts and theories.

Ability to:

- establish effective approaches to enquiry in identified questions and issues
- identify, select and collect quantitative and qualitative evidence using a range of techniques from both primary and secondary sources
- present evidence in cartographic and diagrammatic form
- describe, analyse and evaluate evidence

Options

A number of boards offer two Geography specifications, A and B. In the Edexcel specifications coursework assessment has options of written examination or externally assessed report.

Available unit titles include:

- Applied geographical skills
- Physical systems, processes and patterns
- Changing landforms and their management
- Issues in sustainable development.

Coursework

All specifications include an element of coursework, the formats of which vary. In the OCR specification for AS, a 1000-word report is required evaluating fieldwork undertaken as part of study for the remainder of the qualification. The Edexcel AS specification requires a 2500-word report on a previously approved fieldwork exercise. A2 specifications also contain coursework elements. Contribution to total marks varies. In Edexcel specification B for example, coursework is worth 33% of the AS and 24% of the full A-level.

Course information

Requirements

GCSE Geography may be required at grade C or above; GCSE English is also an advantage.

Goes well with
Any subject; especially Biology, Sociology.

Higher education suitability
Accepted as a strong general A-level; considered by some as a science; usually prescribed for a Geography degree course.

Suggested reading
M. Carr. *Process & Change in Human Geography.* Nelson
R. Collard. *The Physical Geography of Landscape.* Unwin-Hyman
R. Prosser. *Managing Environmental Systems.* Nelson
N. Punnett. *People in the Physical Landscape.* Simon & Schuster

GEOLOGY

If your curiosity leads you to examine the physical characteristics of the planet we live on, you will be a geologist; for Geology is the study of the rocks and minerals that make up the planet Earth, its core and mantle as well as its crust. Far from being a tedious journey into an area that appears to have little relevance to our everyday lives, Geology has many dimensions and can capture the imagination like no other. There are several reasons for this.

First, the study of the earth's origins and its physical evolution, as well as of the life forms to which it gave birth, gives a sense of historical perspective that can permanently affect our perception of the world around us. It is believed that our planet was formed (probably from solidified gas and dust) over 4600 million years ago; but evidence of abundant life is only 570 million years old. The age of reptiles, dominated by the dinosaurs, is much more recent; it eventually gave way to mammals, culminating only two million years ago in the evolution of human life. Since then, the ice ages which shaped so much of our landscapes have come and gone, finally retreating only 11,000 years ago.

Secondly, the earth hides the clues to the most beguiling puzzle confronting us, namely our past. If you would like to know how the planet we live on came into being, how animal and human life evolved; if you want to know about dinosaurs and Neanderthal Man and the era when Britain was joined to mainland Europe or when Africa and south America formed one continent, then you will find the best information from a particular branch of Geology: the study of fossils.

Thirdly, Geology is concerned with what is happening on the earth's surface, or just below it, today. We now know that the crust consists not of a static substance but of a series of mobile slabs, known as 'plates', and that when these plates bump into each other the result, sooner or later, may be a new mountain range, an oceanic trench, an earthquake or an erupting volcano.

Fourthly, the planet we live on is a great provider. It provides us with the minerals with which to fertilise the growth of plants, animals and humans. It gives us the substances that fuel industrial society, from diamonds to roadstone and from uranium to sand. It offers us the oil and oil by-products upon which modern society depends.

Finally, as will by now be evident, Geology is an interdisciplinary subject: its investigations involve Physics, Chemistry, Biology and Mathematics; it informs History and even sometimes anthropology. It also heightens our awareness of one further vital matter: the future of our planet. The rate at which we now exploit the all too finite resources of the world we inhabit not only makes us ever more dependent on geologists and their ability to seek out fresh supplies of raw materials; it also forces us to engage in a debate about our whole relationship with the planet.

Subject criteria

There are no QCA subject criteria for Geology. Geology is offered by OCR and WJEC. The specification described below is that offered by OCR.

Course content

AS

Global tectonics & geological structures

- structure of the earth
- earthquakes
- continental movement
- geological structures

The rock cycle: Processes & products

- sedimentary
- igneous
- metamorphic

Economic & environmental geology

- water supply
- energy resources
- metal deposits
- applied geology

A2

Palaeontology

- preservation of fossils
- morphology
- evolution and extinction
- palaeoenvironments and mode of life

Petrology

- igneous classification and processes
- sedimentary classification and processes
- metamorphic classification and processes

Geological skills

- descriptive, observational and interpretive skills
- use of geological maps and cross sections
- use of photographs and photomicrographs

Coursework

Laboratory and field skills are assessed as coursework components of both AS and A2. In both, laboratory and/or fieldwork is assessed for planning, implementation, analysis and evaluation. A2 coursework is required to demonstrate higher levels of sophistication and skills. In both AS and A-level, coursework contributes 20% of the total marks.

Course Information

Requirements
GCSE Science at grade C or above may be required and will be preferred.

Goes well with
Any subject; especially science subjects, and above all, Biology.

Higher education suitability
Good preparation for courses relating to the land: Agriculture, Ecology, Land & Estate Management; not a course requirement for Geology degrees, for which Biology, Chemistry, Physics or Mathematics are generally preferred.

Suggested reading
J. Bradbury. *Introducing Earth Science.* Blackwell
D. Dixon. *The Practical Geologist.* Aurum
B. Lee. *An Introduction to Geology.* Crowood
A. McLeish. *Geology.* Blackie

GOVERNMENT & POLITICS

Traditionally the studies of Politics and Philosophy were interwoven, the idea of Politics undoubtedly deriving from the way it offers the idealist and the thinker the opportunity for 'action' in the 'real' world, the possibility of influencing the most pressing concerns of our times from nuclear arms to education, health and how much income tax we pay. Today a distinction is made between political science, which examines how government actually works, and political philosophy, which looks at how it should work.

Political science examines past or contemporary politics from two perspectives. On the one hand it looks at political institutions: the laws and customs that provide the framework for government (otherwise known as the constitution), the parties and interest groups that seek to change and influence the government of the day, as well as the political role of the courts, police and judges. Students of political institutions might ask: 'Who really governs Britain – the Queen, the Prime Minister or Parliament?' 'Should so much power be invested in the person of the Prime Minister? (Does the President of the United States have more or less power?)' 'What is the role of the political parties?' 'What influence do trade unions, big business and the media have on government?' 'How would proportional representation affect the way we are governed?' 'Who should appoint our judges?' 'To whom are the police answerable?'

Political scientists also look at political behaviour. This more recent branch of political science, which has grown up alongside Sociology, focuses on the behaviour of men and women involved in the political process. These include not only well-known politicians but also ordinary party members and the study of our own behaviour, both as members of pressure groups and as voters. One modern feature of the study of political behaviour with which most of us are familiar is opinion polling. Students of political behaviour might ask: 'Do opinion polls influence the outcome of elections?'

Behind these issues of contemporary British society (and there are many others concerned with the wider world stage) lie some timeless notions and values, to preserve which throughout history men and women have been prepared to die. This is the arena of the political philosopher. As society and the world change, political ideals need continuous evaluation if they are not to become empty platitudes. A clearer understanding of them will help us to address ideas of nationhood, freedom, democracy, fraternity and social justice, and it is just such matters that form the substance of writers such as Hobbes (*Leviathan*) and Lenin (*What's to be Done?*). The philosophical framework established by such thinkers enables us to tackle such questions as: 'Should membership of a trade union be compulsory (the closed shop)?' 'Does a law that bans incitement to racial hatred infringe the individual's right of free speech?' 'Is it ever right to disobey the law?'

Subject criteria

AS

Reference to current political debate about specified issues

Develop knowledge and understanding within the context of the political system of the UK including local, national and EU dimensions with some comparison with other political systems

A2

Extend knowledge and understanding beyond the UK political system in at least one of the following:

- politics and government of another state

- comparative politics

- international politics

- political ideologies or political thought

- political systems of the EU

Common to AS & A2

The essential characteristics and interrelationships of the legislature, the executive and the judiciary

The adequacy of existing political arrangements for ensuring representative democracy and full participation

The rights and responsibilities of the individual

Ideologies, theories and traditions

Options

The AQA specification has options in A2 where candidates study one of the following: Politics of the USA, Politics of Northern Ireland, Scotland and Wales, Ideas in contemporary British Politics. A2 options are also available in the OCR specification; candidates study Foundations of modern political ideas alongside UK and American politics or US government & politics with UK politics & modern political ideas.

Coursework

There is no coursework in the AQA specification. OCR coursework consists of a personal study of less than 2500 words that is externally marked by the board. Topics should be related to the specification but chosen by the candidate with guidance from the tutor.

Course information

Requirements
GCSE English at grade C or above.

Goes well with
Any subject, especially arts subjects such as History, Geography, English, or social sciences such as Business Studies, Sociology.

Higher education suitability
Accepted as an academic subject for entry to degree courses, particularly social sciences, History or Law; not an essential A-level for those wishing to take Politics in higher education, since all university courses assume no previous tuition in Politics.

Suggested reading
Political journals, eg *Talking Politics*.

I. Budge & I. Crewe. *The New British Politics*. Addison Wesley Longman
B. Goodwin. *Using Political Ideas*. Wiley
A. Grant. *The American Political Process*. Ashgate

HISTORY

What is 'History'? The actual events of the past, from the daily routines of each individual man and woman to the momentous events that affected whole societies, are nothing more than a jumble of unrelated phenomena – existing or happening one moment and gone the next. 'History' is our attempt to make sense of these events and states, to create order out of chaos, to create a unified perspective of the past. Historians do not attempt to do this for everything at once: they subdivide time (prehistoric, classical, mediaeval) and subject matter (political, social, military, educational). They simplify for the sake of an intelligible perspective.

Why does the past interest us so much? The answer is simply that we are unable to see or understand the present without it. The past gives us the points of reference we need to think about the present. Was the Gulf War a just war? Those whose answer to this question is 'yes' depend on a notion of justice formulated by consciousness of past wars (such as the conflict against Hitler).

Writing of all kinds is one of the most important forms of evidence used by historians. It may take many forms, from gravestones (inscriptions yield names and dates) and parish records (teeming with family and social history) to household accounts (economic and social evidence), government edicts, newspapers and, of course, literature.

Much of our understanding of how the Anglo-Saxon tribes lives in pre-Norman England derives from archaeological remains, the best known of which is the Sutton-Hoo burial site. Sometimes the burial is a wet one: Henry VIII's war ship, the *Mary Rose*, located and brought to the surface in 1982, has given us unique insights into Elizabethan life: social, military, culinary and artistic.

Historians must display many of the qualities of detectives as they seek out well-hidden clues, sift evidence, and reach conclusions. Like detectives, they will learn that the past is not just a series of facts; History is also about motivation, rhetoric and emotion.

There has been much debate recently about the way History should be taught to young people. The so-called traditionalists have championed a form of History study that emphasises facts, dates, and the reigns of kings and queens, and that focuses on our island history and stories of empire. Others have sought to present History as a process, as a study of why events occurred, as the key to our future, and to do so in a less parochial way. The protagonists in this debate have often implied that these two views of the study of History are mutually exclusive. It is essential to realise that they are not. If in the end History is in truth a *process* that leads ineluctably to and explains the present, its bricks and mortar are *facts*.

Subject criteria

AS & A2

Develop an understanding of historical terms and contexts

Explore the significance of events, individuals, ideas, attitudes, beliefs, issues and societies

Understand the nature of historical evidence and methods used in analysis and evaluation

Understand and analyse interpretation and representation of historical events

Study a range of historical perspectives, eg cultural, economic and political

Analyse, evaluate, interpret and use historical sources

Use a range of historical concepts in an appropriate manner

A2

Study the history of one or more country/state

Study a substantial element of British history

Study change over a period of time, both long and short term

Draw comparisons between different aspects of the period, society, theme or topic studied

Investigate specific historical questions, problems or issues

Use historical sources, accounts, arguments and interpretations to explain, analyse, synthesise and make judgements

Options

The AQA specification offers 11 alternatives in European and world history for both AS and A2. Examples include Crusading Europe 1046–1225, Social and economic history 1870–1979 and Totalitarian regimes 1848–1956. In British History there are nine alternatives in various periods from 1060–1216 to 1929–98. A similarly wide choice is available in the Edexcel specification. Examples include Russia in revolution 1905–17, Economy and society in the USA 1917–33, The rise of national socialism in Germany to 1933, Votes for women 1880–1918.

Coursework

AQA coursework in AS comprises two essays contributing 30% of the AS qualification or 15% if the work is continued to the full A-level. The A2 coursework is a personal study that is optional and worth a further 20% of the A-level qualification. Edexcel History offers three coursework options: exam only, 15% coursework and 30% coursework. Depending on the option taken there are two pieces of coursework available: AS (1750 words) and A2 (2000 words). Additionally there is an externally marked individual assignment available in A2.

Course information

Requirements
GCSE History at grade C or above if previously studied. Most institutions will also require an A–C grade in English as an additional qualification.

Goes well with
Any arts or social science subject.

Higher education suitability
Good background for a range of courses in higher education; especialy useful for Law, Politics and History itself.

Suggested reading

16th- & 17th-century English & European History
C.S.L. Davies. *Peace, Print & Protestantism: 1450 –1558.* Paladin
A.G.R. Smith. *The Emergence of a Nation State: 1529–1660.* Longman
J. Lotherington (ed.). *Years of Renewal.* Edward Arnold

19th- & 20th-century English & European History
A. Wood. *19th-Century Britian: 1815–1914.* Longman
E.J. Evans. *The Forging of the Modern State: 1760–1870.* Longman
L.W. Cowie & R. Wolfson. *Years of Nationalism.* Edward Arnold
R. Wolfson. *Years of Change.* Edward Arnold

HISTORY OF ART

Long before Art acquired its capital letter, it existed simply as art – a word derived from the Latin *ars*, which simply means skill, or craft. The artist does not have to be a genius, but must be a craftsman.

What is it that distinguishes art from other human activities? The philosopher Plato described it as a form of *play*, emphasising its essentially non-utilitarian nature. For others, art is an attempt to impose order on the chaos and anarchy of nature – and perhaps this was the aim of primitive man when he first painted the interior of his cave. Some of the earliest of such drawings show representations of four-legged creatures resembling bulls; but even in these early attempts to represent nature the cave artists sought to incorporate movement and rhythm into their pictures and to achieve harmony and proportion.

In the present millennium, western art began by modelling itself on the icons and mosaics of Byzantium. It was a Florentine painter, Giotto, who first introduced life and movement into the static Byzantine formula and adopted the freer medium of the *fresco* (painting on wet plaster). The development was taken a stage further by Leonardo da Vinci (1452–1519), inventor, architect, sculptor, engineer, painter and alchemist: the archetypal Renaissance man. He introduced into painting the technique of *chiaroscuro* (the effects of light and shadow) and the principle of *concentration*, whereby the elements of line, shadow and colour within a picture converge on the centre – a principle which became the basis of classical art.

The perfect balance of Italian High Renaissance art held only for a generation before it was overtaken by a new taste for exaggeration, sensational effects (foreshortening, dramatic posture) and religious sensualism – the movement that has come to be known as Mannerism. This in turn developed into the swaggering, showy Baroque style that is chiefly associated with the architecture and sculpture of Bernini in Rome, but that has its counterpart in the paintings of Caravaggio and Rubens. In France it inspired the grandeur of Louis XIV's Versailles at the end of the 17th century, but after Louis' death French artists, bored with a surfeit of glory, turned to the frivolous and flirtatiously erotic style of the Rococo.

The prettiness of the Rococo provoked the serious and austere neo-classicism of the mid-18th century, while this in its turn was swept aside in the early 19th century by the tide of Romanticism. With the advent of Delacroix and Turner, imitation was out and originality was in.

Art history, therefore, is not just the History of Art: it is the history of the human as maker, the history of our visual imagination as it has been affected by a continually changing social, religious and cultural climate.

Subject criteria

There are no QCA subject criteria for History of Art. The subject is offered by AQA only.

Course content

AS

Ways of seeing. Introduction to the methodology and terminology of the subject

The birth and rebirth of western art. Background knowledge of the western tradition from Greek and Roman antiquity to the High Renaissance

Art of the modern world. Background knowledge of modern art, architecture and design from 1850

A2

Historical Study 1

An in-depth study of one topic from:

* ancient Egyptian art and architecture
* Renaissance Florence
* High Renaissance Rome
* Baroque Rome
* English Baroque architecture
* architecture, design and philosophy of galleries and museums
* the Gothic revival

Historical Study 2

An in-depth study of one topic from:

* art and revolution
* 18th and 19th century Japanese prints
* Victorian narrative painting
* the Impressionist period
* women in 20th century art
* painting in Paris 1900–1914
* modern British art 1960 – present day

Coursework

An assignment, of about 3000 words, of the candidate's own choice, assessed by the tutor and moderated by AQA. The work should demonstrate research, analysis, argument and academic presentation. The assignment forms part of the A2 component and contributes 20% of the A-level marks. There is no coursework element in AS.

Course information

Requirements
GCSE English at grade C or above likely to be required.

Goes well with
Any arts-based subject.

Higher education suitability
Good subject to present for any arts degree course.

Suggested reading
E.H. Gombrich. *The Story of Art.* Phaidon
H. Honour & J. Fleming. *A World History of Art.* Macmillan

LATIN AND CLASSICAL GREEK

For centuries the study of Latin has lain at the heart of British education. It no longer enjoys a special status in the curriculum, this is for two reasons. First, it is judged that other subjects enable teachers to pursue equally well many of the educational objectives for which Latin was considered so suitable. Second, school studies today have assumed an additional burden; they must be vocational, practical, 'relevant'.

After this dethronement, Latin has had to argue its case more convincingly. Modern courses have shown that the basic of the language can be mastered quite quickly and that the content of Roman literature may be tackled sooner than was formerly the case. At the same time Latin and its grammar possess a 'relevance' which must not be forgotten: its clarity and symmetry, which is lacking in English, is a model for understanding most Western languages; and close analysis of complex Latin sentences with their logical construction should inoculate students forever against sloppiness in the use of their own language. The training they receive in linguistic accuracy, clarity and coherence will benefit them in whatever career they follow.

Though Greek was subordinate to Latin in the traditional curriculum, it has the greater claim to importance: the Romans borrowed from the Greeks and imitated their writings. Anyone wishing to tap the source of European thought and literature must, therefore, go to the Greeks.

In spite of appearances, Greek is easier than Latin, its looser sentence structure is more akin to that of modern languages; its freshness, flexibility and subtlety were the envy of the Romans. Greek has provided scholarship, science and technology with an international vocabulary of -ologies and -onomies and is a key to understanding abstract terminology.

The main legacy of Classical Greek is its literature. The oldest of its 'classics' – Homer's *Iliad* and *Odyssey* – are as fresh today as they were to the ancient Greeks. Homer created a model of epic poetry which was later to inspire Vergil, Dante and Milton.

Even after its military defeat by Sparta in 404, intellectual life in Athens continued unabated. The 3rd century was an age of political decline, but this was the age of Plato and Aristotle, its greatest philosophers. Plato turned away from politics to philosophy, in disgust at the trial and execution of his master Socrates under a democratic regime. It is ironic that many of Athens' most influential writers – Thucydides, Xenophon, Plato, Aristotle – were out of sympathy with the democracy that produced them and which is Athens' most lasting political legacy. To read Plato is to confront the major problems of human existence. Indeed, at every stage the reader of Greek encounters issues that are alive today.

Subject criteria

AS & A2

Extend knowledge of vocabulary and linguistic structures through reading and studying prescribed texts in the original language

The different ways in which ideas are expressed in English and in Latin/Classical Greek

Understand at least 550 lines of verse and/or prose from prescribed texts

Understand and appreciate literature and have a critical awareness of its meaning, the authors' purposes and literary techniques; literary, social and historical contexts

A2

Understand a further 550 lines of verse and/or prose from prescribed texts

Understand and translate unprepared material in the original language in both prose and verse

Linguistic content

Classical Greek: language of the 5th and 4th centuries BC

Accidence: the definite article, declension of nouns and adjectives, formation of adverbs, comparison of adjectives and adverbs, pronouns and pronominal adjectives, verbs of all standard types, cardinal and ordinal numbers, prepositions and prepositional prefixes.

Syntax: standard patterns of case usage, negation, direct statement, indirect statement, description, purpose, result, conditional, causal, temporal, indefinite, fearing, prevention and precaution, concessive, other uses of the infinite, other participial, comparison, impersonal verbs, verbal nouns and adjectives, classical Greek accentuation.

Latin: language of 1st century BC and 1st century AD

Accidence: declension of nouns and adjectives, formation of adverbs, comparison of adjectives and adverbs, pronouns and pronominal adjectives, verbs of all standard types, cardinal and ordinal numbers, prepositions and prepositional prefixes.

Syntax: standard patterns of case usage, negation, direct statement, indirect statement, description, purpose, result, conditional, causal, temporal, indefinite, fearing, prevention and precaution, extended oratio obliqua, use of gerund and gerundive.

Options

The AQA specification offers a choice from prescribed topics and prescribed books of verse. OCR offers ten options in the literature units of both AS and A2 with some banned combinations for those going on to the full A-level.

Coursework

There is no coursework assessment in either the AQA or the OCR specification.

Course information

Requirements

A minimum of GCSE grade C in either Latin or Greek as appropriate; grades A or B will be preferred and may be required.

Goes well with

Any subject.

Higher education suitability

Highly regarded by universities for any humanities degree; introduces the major literary genres (historical writing, epic, lyric, rhetoric) and equips students of modern languages with an essential technical vocabulary.

Suggested reading

Greek
A. Bowle. *Aristophanes: Myth, Ritual & Comedy.* CUP
M. Finley. *The Ancient Greeks.* Pelican

Latin
R. Mellor. *The Roman Historians.* Routledge
R. Ogilvie. *Roman Literature & Society.* Pelican
D. Stockton. *Cicero: A Political Biography.* OUP

LAW

What we call 'the law' has four separate aspects. First, it is a series of rules governing our social and public behaviour. In England there are two sources for these rules: Parliament and the courts. Parliament is the supreme law-making authority and has the power to enact what legislation it chooses. However, it is incumbent on the courts to interpret parliamentary law, known as Statute Law, and to apply it to the individual cases they deal with. The decisions made by the courts in this way themselves become law.

Secondly, the law is administered by a series of interlocking institutions that include the courts of justice (civil and criminal), tribunals and enquiry commissions as well as other bodies with legal roles to play in our society such as the Directorate of Public Prosecutions, the police, the Bar Council and the Law Society.

Thirdly, the law is a profession – two professions in fact: that of the barrister and that of the solicitor. Most of those who earn their living by the law are solicitors, and it is usually to a solicitor that a member of the public will go for help or advice. It is now normal for solicitors to specialise in chosen branches of law (such as crime, commercial, employment, trusts). Barristers are even more likely to specialise in a narrow field of law but they also have a role that to date, solicitors do not have: representing their clients, they may stand up in and address any court in the land, a part of their work known as 'advocacy'. This is the role in which most people tend to imagine barristers, but in practice most of their work is desk-bound and not dissimilar to that of solicitors (who may themselves practice advocacy in lower courts). This traditional division of the legal profession into two branches is currently under review and those interested in law should be aware of likely developments.

Finally, Law is a subject of study. In fact, it holds an almost unique position in being simultaneously a vocational and an academic discipline. Whilst for many learning about Law is akin to preparing for any other professional qualification (such as accountancy, banking or surveying), for centuries it has also been a source of intense interest to the philosophically minded. The study of Law addresses many social and ethical problems. 'Is there such a thing as a justifiable defence of murder?' 'How far should the law of the land guarantee free speech to those whose statements stir up racial prejudice?' 'Should the consumption of alcohol be the subject of legal constraint?' The general issues that lie behind these questions are timeless; the answers are of immediate concern to all societies today. Indeed, a society may be fairly judged by its laws and by the attitudes of its members to law. Law teaches us to apply universal principles to practical problems and for that reason alone is as useful a subject of study as any other academic discipline.

Subject criteria

AS & A2

Develop a knowledge and understanding of selected areas of English law

Develop an understanding of legal method and reasoning

Develop techniques of logical thinking and problem solving by applying legal rules

Develop the ability to communicate legal arguments with reference to appropriate legal authority

Develop a critical awareness of the changing nature of law in society

Study of:

- legal structures, eg court structures
- legal processes, eg law making
- legal issues, eg law reform
- legal methods, eg precedent

A2

Study one or more areas of substantive law in depth

Options

At A-level the OCR specification allows specialisation in one of three areas in A2: Criminal law, Law of contract and Law of torts. The AQA specification has optional subjects for two of the A2 units, eg Criminal law or Contract law for Unit 4.

Coursework

The maximum internal assessment weighting for A-level Law is 20%. Neither the AQA and OCR specifications have a coursework element.

Course information

Requirements

Normally GCSE English at grade C or above.

Goes well with

Any subject.

Higher education suitability

Suitable for those wishing to pursue Business Studies or a social science at university or college; not a requirement for those wishing to take a Law degree, and many Law faculties prefer you not to have taken the A-level.

Suggested reading

D. Bloy. *Principles of Criminal Law.* Cavendish

T. Downes. *Textbook on Contract.* Blackstone

C. Elliot & F. Quinn. *English Legal System.* Addison Wesley Longman

M. Jones. *Textbook on Torts.* Blackstone

G. Slapper & D. Kelly. *Principles of the English Legal System.* Butterworth

MATHEMATICS

Probably more than any other subject in the curriculum, Mathematics elicits strong feelings from students; they tend either to enjoy it enormously or to be intensely wary of it. If you have a reasonable aptitude for Mathematics and if it is approached correctly the subject can be rewarding, enjoyable and useful. Indeed, it has one special advantage: it is just about the only academic discipline that does not involve a substantial volume of factual knowledge. It is often said that Mathematics is the application of a finite number of methods to an infinite number of problems. A good understanding of the principles involved, together with practice in solving these recurring types of problems, will make a successful mathematician.

Mathematics is a group of related sciences:

Arithmetic: numerical calculations such as addition, subtraction, multiplication and division

Mechanics: the study of forces and how physical objects either move (such as the working of a nutcracker) or stay still (an erect building)

Statistics: the study of how frequently events occur and how likely they are to occur

Algebra: the use of symbols, such as x, to represent numbers in generalised arithmetical operations and relationships

Calculus: the means we use to calculate movement and change, such as how fast cars travel as well as their ratio of acceleration

Geometry: the properties, relationships and measurement of points, lines, curves and surfaces

Trigonometry: the properties of trigonometric functions and their use in measuring the sides and angles of triangles

Decision Mathematics: Mathematics in the 'real' world.

Mechanics and Statistics are sometimes known as 'Applied Mathematics'; Algebra, Calculus, Geometry and Trigonometry form part of 'Pure Mathematics'.

Mathematics has numerous applications. It is used to solve practical problems in all fields of architecture and engineering. It is required in business: accountancy, Economics and many other aspects of business demand a certain degree of numeracy. It plays a part in Philosophy: Plato believed in an ideal world of perfect numbers, and saw the material world as striving to attain this without completely succeeding – as is demonstrated by the fact that a perfect circle does not exist in the real world.

Subject criteria

Maths is a sequential subject in that there is a progression of material through all levels. The subject criteria build on GCSE through AS to A-level.

In the table below material in *italics* represents that required to take the subject through to A-level.

AS and *A2*

Algebra & functions

Laws of indices, surds, quadratic functions and graphs, simultaneous equations, linear and quadratic inequalities, algebraic manipulation of polynomials *including simplification of rational expressions: factorising, cancelling and algebraic division*, functions *including rational functions, the Remainder Theorem*

Coordinate Geometry in the (x,y) plane

Equation of a straight line, *coordinate geometry of the circle, Cartesian and parametric equations of curves*

Sequences & series

Sequences *including those generated by a simple recurrence of the form* $x_{n+1} = f(x_n)$, Arithmetic series, the sum of finite geometric series, *Binomial expansion of* $(1+x)^n$, *Binomial series for any rational n*

Trigonometry

Radian measure, Sine, cosine and tangent, *Secant, cosecant and cotangent,* $\tan\theta = \sin\theta/\cos\theta$, $\sin^2\theta + \cos^2\theta = 1$ *and its equivalents, double angle formulae,* solution of simple trigonometric equations

Exponentials & logarithms

e^x and its graph, *exponential growth and decay, ln x and its graph, solution of equations of the form* $a^x = b$

Differentiation

The derivative of $f(x)$ as the gradient of the tangent to the graph of $y = f(x)$ at a point and other aspects, differentiation of x^n, e^x, $\ln x$ and their sums and differences, *differentiation of sin x, cos x, tan x, and their sums and differences; application* of differentiation to gradients, *tangents and normals; differentiation using the product, quotient and chain rules and by the use of dy/dx = 1/(dx/dy), differentiation of simple functions defined implicitly or parametrically, formation of simple differential equations*

Integration

Indefinite integration as the reverse of differentiation, integration of x^n, e^x, $1/x$, *sin x, cos x,* evaluation of definite integrals, *evaluation of volume of revolution, simple cases by substitution and integration by parts, using partial fractions, analytical solution of simple first order differential equations*

Numerical methods

Location of roots of $f(x) = 0$, approximate *solution of equations using simple iterative methods, numerical integration of functions*

Vectors

Vectors in 2 and 3 dimensions, magnitude, algebraic operations of vector addition and multiplication position vectors, the scalar product

Options

Mathematics is offered in the following titles: AS Maths, Further Maths, Pure Maths, Statistics, Mechanics and Applied Maths, A-level Maths, Further Maths, Pure Maths and Statistics.

The Edexcel specification offers 20 mathematics units that, subject to laws of combination and dependency, can be combined to qualify for the titles above. Some titles have optional units, others are predefined. AQA offers two Maths specifications, A and B. In the same manner as described above the AQA specification B offers 23 maths units available under similar constraints as described for Edexcel.

Coursework

The Edexcel specification has a coursework component in the Statistics units for both AS and A2. Projects are of a topic of the candidates' own choosing and are worth 25% of the mark for the unit. There is no assessment by coursework in AQA specification B.

Course information

Requirements
Normally GCSE Maths at grade A or B is required, although some institutions will accept grade C.

Goes well with
Any subject; especially useful for Economics (Statistics option) and Physics (Mechanics option).

Higher education suitability
A required A-level for almost all Engineering disciplines, and for certain courses in Business Studies or Economics; relevant to almost any science or social science degree.

Suggested reading

Heinemann's textbooks in AS/A Mathematics support the Edexcel specification.

J.A. Paulos. *Innumeracy.* Penguin

MEDIA STUDIES

Our perception of the external world is very significantly governed by the media. Most of us read newspapers and magazines, watch television and videos, listen to the radio, go to the theatre and cinema. We do so in order to be informed and entertained; in order actively to learn or to be the passive recipient of media messages – from weather forecasters to advertisers, from politicians to preachers. It is very important that we understand this powerful giant that we call the media and learn as much as we can about it. It is useful to known how its different forms, such as television or newspapers, work in a technical sense; it is essential to be aware of how the media controls our view of the world; it is important to know something about the organisations and interest groups that run it.

The technical aspects of the media can be the most fun to study. How do you make a video or produce a colour poster? How are newspapers and magazines produced and distributed so punctually day in and day out? Many skills are employed and brought together to achieve this feat: writing, taking photographs, designing, using a computer, printing. Each branch of the media requires its own special skills and disciplines – all united for the dissemination of information and ideas, for the gentle art of persuasion and for the enlargement of our view of the world we live in.

We must, however, be an intelligent audience. We must be aware that the media is not only useful; it is also powerful and, in the wrong hands, dangerous. We need to know who controls the various media we allow to influence our lives. Most forms of media exist to make money. Those who work in the media also seek to shape the way we see the world we live in – in the process controlling us in some measure. All forms of media, from a Hollywood western to a daily newspaper, give expression to moral, social and political values. There is nothing wrong with this; indeed films and newspapers would not be very interesting if they didn't; but we must learn to recognise the way in which these values affect the way life is depicted in these films and newspapers and so also how we, the audience, see and judge the 'real world'.

There is nothing new about these sorts of issues. All poets, dramatists and writers throughout the centuries have been exponents of the media. There is, however, something new about the extent to which the reality of modern life and our perception of it is linked with the modern media. And there is something almost frightening about the pace of technical change that affects the media. But interactive CD-ROMs, games of 'laserquest', satellite television are here to stay: it is better to understand and control them than to be merely their passive spectators.

Subject criteria

There are no QCA subject criteria for Media Studies. The subject is offered by OCR and incorporates the following.

AS

Foundation production: Coursework

Comparative textual study: TV/radio

Comparative textual study: Film

Comparative textual study: Print

A2

Advanced production: Coursework

Critical research study

Media issues & debates

Options

AS candidates choose two of the three comparative textual studies: TV/radio, film or print. Texts for the AS modules must be of the same genre and are approved by the school/college. A wide choice of topics is available for the A2 externally assessed modules, eg:

- Critical research study:
    Girl power and popular culture
    Daytime TV
    Media moguls

- Media issues & debates:
    British TV soap opera
    Censorship and film
    Women's and men's lifestyle magazines

Coursework

The AS and A-level coursework units differ in the degree of direction expected of the tutor. The foundation production is 1500–2000 words and the advanced production 2500 words. Examples of subjects include: the opening sequence of a film, the closing sequence of a soap opera, a TV advertisement. Coursework contributes 40% of the marks to both AS and A-level.

Course information

Requirements
GCSE English at grade C or above will be required.

Goes well with
Any arts or humanities subject but Communication Studies should be avoided due to excessive overlap.

Higher education suitability
Media Studies has a substantial academic content and is an acceptable A-level for those seeking admission to degree courses in arts subjects.

Suggested reading
M. Alvarado. *Learning the Media.* Macmillan

MODERN FOREIGN LANGUAGES

The reputation of the British people as bad linguists is largely deserved. That this is so may in some measure be due to circumstance rather than innate linguistic deficiency. What need had the English to learn the languages of other nations when so many others spoke theirs?

The answer is supplied by the French saying, that 'A man who speaks two languages is two men'. Indeed, one of the most exhilarating things about speaking another language is a sense of a dimension lacking to those who only speak one. Mastering another tongue enables you to become acquainted with another way of thinking and another culture: it opens up a new world of enriching experiences, feeling and being. At the same time the ability to speak another language brings a series of purely practical benefits; and it enables us to communicate more freely and form relationships with more people in more parts of the world. In a world where the technology of communication brings everyone closer together such a skill is essential.

The teaching of languages reflects this twin aspect of a foreign language. In the past the emphasis was on acquiring a correct literary style, on learning complex grammar and on reading and understanding classical literary texts. Today these elements are still there but are counterbalanced by some of the more practical aspects of language work, such as understanding the way the language is written and spoken in everyday situations and how to speak it oneself. Indeed, learning how to communicate verbally lies at the heart of most modern language study today.

French is the language of our nearest neighbour. Spanish is a rapidly growing world language, whose sphere of influence now extends from South and Central America into the US. Russian is the key to eastern Europe, while German, besides laying claim to Goethe and Thomas Mann, is the language of the most powerful industrial nation in modern Europe. When choosing between languages, however, it is best to be guided by the heart. You must have a liking for the people who speak the language, their countries and cultures.

It is a mistake to think that studying, say, French, must lead to a career as an interpreter or courier. It can be applied in many areas: cultural, commercial, academic and social. Finally, learning a foreign language is much the best way of coming to terms with analysis of grammar. In the process of learning how another language is 'inflected' – that is to say, the ways in which the words change to convey different meanings – you are presented with the structures of grammar in an orderly and graspable way. So learning French or German or Russian can be a means to a better understanding of *English*. 'They little know of England who only England know.'

Subject criteria

AS

Understanding of the society, culture and heritage of countries/communities whose language is studied

Listen and respond to a variety of authentic spoken sources

Read and respond to a variety of written texts

Demonstrate flexibility when communicating in speech and writing

Use appropriate registers in both spoken and written information

Organise facts and ideas, present explanations, opinions and information in both speech and writing

Understand and apply the grammatical system of the language studied as per AS specification*

Transfer meaning from the modern foreign language into English

A2

Understand the cultural aspects above in greater depth, demonstrating a higher level of critical awareness

Use the language to analyse, hypothesise, argue a case, justify, persuade, rebut, develop arguments and present viewpoints in speech and writing

Demonstrate a capacity for critical thinking, relationships within the subject and breadth of perception

Understand and apply the grammatical system of the language studied as per A-level specification and use a wider range of vocabulary**

Transfer meaning from English into the modern foreign language

* Example for French AS level:
Verbs: Regular and irregular, modes of address, impersonal forms, dependent infinitives, perfect infinitive, negative forms, interrogative forms, tenses

**Example for French A-level:
Verbs: Those listed for AS level plus future perfect tense, conditional perfect tense, passive voice: all tenses, subjunctive mood: imperfect

Options
Modern Foreign Languages are available in the following subject areas.

Arabic	German	Modern Greek	Portuguese
Bengali	Gujarati	Modern Hebrew	Russian
Chinese	Hindi	Panjabi	Spanish
Dutch	Italian	Persian	Turkish
French	Japanese	Polish	Urdu

Options are available on the style of assessment of the spoken component of the examination, eg whether assessed internally or externally. The coursework component may also be optional. The Edexcel specification offers five main pathways depending on the main interests of the candidate, eg literary or cultural.

Coursework

The OCR specification has a coursework option for Culture and society taken in A2 and worth 15% of the total mark. One or two pieces of written work are submitted on a literary or cultural theme. The Edexcel coursework option requires two pieces of work of the candidate's own choice, again covering the cultural dimension. Again the coursework option is part of A2 study and is worth 15% of the total A-level mark.

Course information

Requirements
GCSE at grade C or above will be required if the prospective student is not a native speaker; many institutions will require grades A or B.

Goes well with
Any subject.

Higher education suitability
A modern language degree course in the language taken at A-level; other languages studied from scratch; Business Studies; arts degrees in general.

MUSIC

Unlike some arts, music appears to owe little to nature; yet early forms of the art were undoubtedly vocal and almost certainly took the form of stylised renderings of sounds expressing the full range of human emotions – from fear to adoration. Music has the power to awaken instincts more elemental than any evoked by those arts that appear more obviously to imitate life, such as painting or sculpture. For the Greeks, who gave us the word 'music', it meant 'belonging to the muses'.

However, like most non-European music today, Greek music was relatively unsophisticated, its essential feature being melody. Just as the development of painting owes much to the discovery of perspective, it was the development of harmony (the clothing of a melodic line with chords) that heralded in Europe the flowering of our musical heritage and, more importantly, that singles it out from the music of any other culture at any other time. What started life in the 10th century as simple unison developed into elaborate part-writing and polyphony and reached its crescendo towards the end of the 16th century in the choral writing, motets, madrigals and cappella Masses of Palestrina in Italy and Byrd in England. It then found perhaps its most perfect expression in the classical period of Mozart, Beethoven and Schubert.

The history of European music in the last 400 years may be thought of in terms of overlapping cycles, as the Classical period gave way to the Romanticism of Weber, Berlioz, Wagner, Chopin, Mendelssohn and Tchaikovsky, composers who sought to develop harmony further and make it more ardently expressive; after Wagner, this mood in turn gave way to the anti-romantic spirit of Schoenberg, Stravinsky and Bartok. Each cycle has it periods of growth, maturity and decline and their boundaries are never hard: Elgar, Vaughan Williams, Walton and Britten are as much products of the 20th century as the modernists, Boulez and Stockhausen; so are the American musical, jazz and rock.

A study of Music should lead to an understanding of its inner mechanisms, of what it is that makes a succession of pleasing tones. All sounds that pass for music conform to principles described in such terms as Binary or Ternary form, Sonata form, Rondo form, Variations or Fugue; and the musical patterns these terms describe form the basis of nearly every musical creation from the mediaeval troubadours' songs to 20th-century pop and rock.

Finally, Music is not just for study. It is also to be made afresh. Musical composition is the result of inspiration and hard work. There are in a sense no rules to composition, though many have certainly been laid down. The results will inspire us, educate us, entertain us, perhaps send us off to battle, probably bury us.

Subject criteria

AS & A2

Expressive use of musical elements, structures and resources through:

* interpreting musical ideas
* creating and developing musical ideas using innovative and/or established musical techniques

Critical judgement of musical elements, structures and resources through:

* analysing, evaluating and reflecting on own and others' work

Gain a depth of understanding of two contrasting ideas of study across time and/or place – at least one from western classical tradition

Gain a breadth of understanding by placing the selected areas within a broader musical perspective

Develop and apply knowledge, understanding and specialist vocabulary to:

* the use of musical elements including harmonic progressions and relationships
* musical structures including established forms
* appropriate notations including staff notation
* relationship between music and its context

Due regard to the interdependence of skills, knowledge and understanding encouraging the integration of performing, composing and responding

A2

Demonstrate more finely discriminating aural perception

Improved range, control and application of specific techniques and conventions

Increased stylistic awareness in performance and composing

Increased depth of study in one of the areas selected for AS

One further area of study

More extensive connection of different areas of knowledge and aspects of musical activities

Apply knowledge and understanding to unfamiliar music

Options

Multiple options are available in both Performing and Composing modules. In the Edexcel unit, Developing musical ideas, candidates submit a free composition from a range of topics including Romantic miniatures, Popular song and Club dance and hip hop.

Coursework

Specifications include practical assessment and coursework assessed both internally and externally. In the OCR specification Performing is assessed by visiting examiner and Composing by teacher-assessed folio; the two elements together are worth two-thirds of the marks for both AS and A-level.

Course information

Requirements

GCSE Music at grade C or above is desirable but not essential for candidates with alternative and appropriate musical backgrounds.

Goes well with

Any subject.

Higher education suitability

Accepted as an approved A-level subject both for matriculation purposes and as a means of meeting the course requirements of a very large number of degree courses.

Suggested reading
A. Copland. *What to Listen for in Music.* Penguin
K. Ganzi. *The Encyclopaedia of Musical Theatre.* Blackwell
J. Rushton. *A Concise History of Classical Music.* Thames & Hudson
E. Taylor. *The AB Guide to Music Theory.* ABRSM

PHILOSOPHY

Our English word 'philosophy' comes from the Greek words meaning (roughly) 'a love of wisdom'. The subject has been studied since ancient Greek times, and some of the best-known philosophers – Plato, Socrates and Aristotle – lived in Greece between about 460 and 320 BC. Many of the topics discussed and written about in ancient Greece are likely to appear in any Philosophy course today. The Greeks asked questions such as, 'What is the definition of the "good life", and how should we go about living it?' They also wondered about the nature of reality: are things really as they seem, and how is truth to be discovered? They asked themselves about the meaning of life and the universe, and whether a god or gods exist. Part of their job was to teach their pupils how to argue effectively, so they tried to define the nature of logical argument. And they were also very interested in Politics, wanting to know what was the most legitimate form of Government, and how far the state was entitled to interfere with the liberty of the individual.

So, what is Philosophy? Philosophy makes a detailed study of the language people use, the concepts they apply to what they experience, and the reasoning they use to build up theories. For instance, a lawyer might talk about the 'evidence' that 'proved' a client 'not guilty', or might claim that, though guilty, the client did not know what he was doing for some reason, and so was not 'responsible'. A philosopher of law would ask different questions: 'How do you measure evidence to decide when it amounts to proof?' 'Do lawyers use the same standards of proof as scientists and, if not, why not?' 'What exactly is a "reasonable" doubt, as opposed to an unreasonable one?' 'How is the word "responsible" being used?' Some psychologists and sociologists have argued that people are so controlled by their heredity, upbringing and surroundings that they can never be free to choose to do anything. So is anyone responsible for what they do?

More than anything else, Philosophy is a style of asking rather odd-seeming questions and then applying its own techniques of reasoning and analysis to try to answer them. Once this philosophical method has been mastered, it can be applied to almost any area of human study, and so there are very many philosophies: of religion, of law, of science, of mind, of language, of morals and politics, of logic and so on.

One modern philosopher, Stuart Hampshire, wrote that most Philosophy was concerned with the words 'know', 'true', 'exist', 'same', 'cause' and 'good'. Most contemporary philosophers would want to add some extras to this list (particularly, 'reason', 'mind' and 'meaning'), but Hampshire's list gives a fair idea of what would be studied in a Philosophy course at a British school or university today.

Subject criteria

There are no QCA subject criteria for Philosophy. The subject is offered by AQA only.

Course content

AS

Theory of knowledge: Empiricism and rationalism, knowledge and justification, knowledge and scepticism, knowledge of the external world

Either Moral philosophy: Normative ethics, practical ethics, meta-ethics: cognitivism and non-cognitivism

Or Philosophy of religion: Meaning and justification of religious concepts, arguments for the existence of God, the implications of God's existence

Candidates demonstrate a critical awareness on the content, structure and use of argument in one text taken from:

Plato *The Republic*

Descartes *Meditations*

Marx & Engels *The German Ideology*

Sartre *Existentialism & Humanism*

A2

Either Philosophy of mind: Approaches to mentality and the nature of mind, the mind and body problem, knowledge of self and self-conciousness

Or Political philosophy: Political ideologies, freedom, law, authority

Or Philosophy of science: Scientific method, nature of scientific development, scientific knowledge and the aims of science, the objectivity of science, natural and social science

Candidates demonstrate a critical awareness on the content, structure and use of argument in one text taken from:

Aristotle *Nicomachean Ethics*

Hume *An Enquiry Concerning Human Understanding*

Mill *On Liberty*

Nietzsche *Beyond Good & Evil*

Russell *The Problems of Philosophy*

Ayer *Language, Truth & Logic*

Coursework

There is no coursework element in AQA Philosophy but Unit 6 of A2 takes the form of an extended essay based on student research written under supervised conditions. The essay should assess the contributions of two philosophers to a major debate or the impact of one on the development of a philosophical theme.

Course information

Requirements

GCSE English at grade C or above likely to be required.

Goes well with

Any subject.

Higher education suitability

Philosophy develops skills that are highly useful and transferable; there is no discipline or profession that does not benefit from the systematic thought processes and clarity of expression that Philosophy develops.

Suggested reading

J. Gaarder. *Sophie's World.* Phoenix
M. Hollis. *An Invitation to Philosophy.* Blackwell

PHYSICAL EDUCATION

Sport channels, but also triggers, our violent natures. It has been said that modern sport provides an acceptable outlet for our aggression – a replacement for war no less. Yet it is also associated with public disorder.

Sport provides careers and livelihoods for many and for a few competitors success brings fame to equal that of statesmen and pop stars. For many others the sporting world provides steady if less glamorous jobs as coaches, managers, administrators, physiotherapists, promoters, ticket-sellers and journalists.

Sport helps us to teach young people how to learn society's rules, how to grow up, how to respect each other, and develops qualities we value such as concentration, courage, determination.

It is not surprising that such a pervasive human activity has become a 'subject', studied in universities, colleges – and now sixth forms.

For many the most important thing to learn is how to improve performance: how we learn sporting techniques, how the brain and body acquire and memorise skills. Closely related to this is Sport Science: a study of fitness and of the effects of exercise on our muscles, heart and oxygen consumption; how diet affects our performance; how exercise improves our long-term health; how principles of biomechanics, linear kinematics, angular motion and anatomy affect sport techniques; how muscles are subject to and may be explained by the laws of linear and angular motion.

Sporting activity also raises important questions of psychology. How are sportsmen and women motivated and how do they control and exploit the anxieties that competition generates? What is and what causes competitiveness? What is the nature of the aggression associated with sporting activity? What motivates competitors? What are the factors that make for a good captain and 'team spirit'?

Sport can also be looked at in its historical context, as it developed from its roots in pre-industrial England – the semi-organised activities of the public holiday, often associated with drinking and gambling, and the 'sportsmanship' later nurtured in the public schools – to the modern commercial spectacle, financed by sponsorship and television.

The sociology of sport comes not far behind. How do social class and race affect the growth of sport and how do they impinge on its organisation and practice? What is the relationship between gender and sport? What part does the media play in modern sport? Why is sport associated with certain types of deviance, such as hooliganism and drug-taking?

Subject criteria

AS

Factors influencing performance in a variety of physical activities

Improvement of performance through analysis and practice

AS & A2

Analysis and evaluation of practical performance from a selection of games, gymnastics, dance, athletics, outdoor pursuits and swimming

Analysis and evaluation of physical factors affecting performance

- applied anatomy

- principles and methods of training

- exercise physiology

- energy systems

Analysis and evaluation of determinants of skilled performance through learning, practice and cognitive factors influencing skilled performance

Analysis and evaluation of contemporary issues influencing performance and participation including social, moral and cultural aspects

A2

The relationship between theoretical concepts such as the social and cultural bases of sport and recreation and how these inform and explain physical education programmes, elite and recreative sport

Compare UK/European trends with those of different cultures such as North America, Kenya and Argentina

Options

Edexcel coursework has options of 13 individual activities, eg athletics and golf; ten team activities, eg rugby and soccer; and four racket activities, eg tennis. AS coursework has options of a practical assessment of two activities in a competitive situation or a research project. A2 coursework has the options of a practical assessment or investigative study. As with Edexcel, the AQA specification offers alternatives on coursework modules both at AS and A2. Again the options are that of practical coursework based around personal performance or an investigative research project. In A2 the AQA project may be based on artistic, individual or team sporting activities.

Coursework

In both the Edexcel and AQA specifications coursework is required for both AS and A2. Some detail of these is given under *Options* above. Additionally the AQA A2 specification includes coursework that draws on the knowledge from the four theory modules in an analysis and evaluation of a live or recorded performance.

Course information

Requirements
No specific passes at GCSE are likely to be required but normal admission for A-level programmes will apply.

Goes well with
Science subjects generally.

Higher education suitability
Candidates not wishing to pursue sports study to higher education should check the acceptability of this A-level for other courses.

Suggested reading
P. Beashel & J. Taylor. *Advanced Studies in Physical Education & Sport.* Nelson

R. Davis et al. *Physical Education & the Study of Sport.* Mosby

PHYSICS

Physics is the study of the physical world. The most exciting research looks back into the far distant past as well as into the future. Elementary particle physicists are trying to describe the instant of the Big Bang that started our universe. Nuclear physicists are just beginning to make controlled nuclear fusion a reality, recreating the process of the sun's energy production that will solve many of our future energy problems.

Physics began at the point when people started to ask why things happened and experimented to test their ideas. As is often the case, the story starts with the Greeks who were postulating laws about the physical world more than 2000 years ago. Archimedes formulated his law about levers – explaining why it is that a walnut cannot be cracked open by the pressure of human fingers but opens easily to the pressure of the same fingers using the levers of a nutcracker. Today, this may seem obvious. At the same time, however, Aristotle stated a law of motion and described a model that showed how the planets moved round the Earth. This was held to be true until hundreds of years later when Newton showed that the planets, including the Earth, circled the sun. Thus does our understanding of the truth progress: observations lead to hypotheses that are tested by experiment. Those that survive the test may be turned into laws that are used to predict other likely behaviour; but they survive only until they themselves break down: even Newton's brilliant descriptions of our world are found to break down at high speeds and in high gravitational fields. At the beginning of this century, Einstein postulated laws that still appear revolutionary today: he predicted that clocks will slow down when moving at high speed or run at different rates when going up and down a tall building in a lift. Only time will tell whether Einstein's theories will be superseded rather than refined.

The beauty of Physics is its simplicity. As the most 'fundamental' of the sciences it has laws of enormous strength and scope, the laws and principles to which it gives rise being few in comparison with the explanations they allow. That light changes direction in a changing medium explains a mirage over a hot road and the formation of a rainbow, as well as having a practical application in slow-motion photography. Galvani suspended frogs' legs from iron before cooking them and noticed that they twitched whenever they touched a copper nail: luckily he found this interesting and the discovery of the battery ensued.

Physics will be central to our lives in the future. It is in no small measure because of advances in electronics that our lives are now run by computers and our factories by robots. What will holography mean for our leisure time in the future? Will every home have the film of its choice projecting three-dimensional images in its living room?

Subject criteria

AS

Mechanics:

- vectors
- kinematics
- dynamics

Momentum & energy: **OR**   Waves

- momentum concepts
- energy concepts
- molecular kinetic theory

Electricity:

- current
- electromotive force and potential difference
- resistance
- DC circuits

Nuclear physics: **OR**   Quantum physics

- probing matter   • photons
- ionising radiation   • matter

A2 – All the above including all options plus

Electricity:

- capacitance

Nuclear physics:

- energy

Waves:

- oscillations

Fields:

- force fields
- magnetic effects of currents

Options

OCR offer two specifications for Physics. Specification A offers a number of options for one of the A2 units, these being Cosmology, Health physics, Materials, Nuclear physics or Telecommunications. Practical examination or coursework options are also available for both AS and A2. Edexcel also offers two specifications, one of which is Salters Horners Physics, which takes a functional approach based on application of the subject in diverse areas, eg the operation of a CD player and product testing of chocolate biscuits.

Coursework

The OCR coursework assesses four skills: planning, implementing, analysis and evaluation. Skills may be assessed in separate practical exercises or as a single investigation. Whilst suggested topics are available, the area covered by the coursework is optional to the candidate or to the tutor. The Edexcel Salters Horners specification offers assessment of two lab-based practicals and an off-site visit for AS and a two-week individual project in A2.

Course information

Requirements
Normally grades C or above in GCSE Physics or Combined Science, together with Maths.

Goes well with
Science subjects such as Chemistry, Biology, Mathematics, Computing.

Higher education suitability
Necessary for Physics, Mathematics and Engineering degrees; useful for Medicine, Computing and degree courses requiring proof of scientific ability.

Suggested reading
J. Breihaupt. *Understanding Physics for Advanced Level.* Stanley Thornes
T. Duncan. *Advanced Physics.* John Murray
Cambridge Modular Science Series. CUP
Salters Horners Advanced Physics Course Materials. Heinemann Education

PSYCHOLOGY

The word 'Psychology' suggests to many people ideas of mental illness, odd behaviour and dreams. Although there are clinical psychologists who (without the use of drugs available to psychiatrists) treat patients with mental disorders, these are rare: most professionals in this field are concerned with normal states of mind. Indeed, one of the aims of Psychology is to establish precisely what counts as 'normal' and by implication 'abnormal' behaviour. It is also concerned with the way in which we assimilate the external world.

Psychology is a study of human behaviour. It seeks to answer questions about ourselves: 'Why do some people smoke?' 'Why are some people more competitive at sport than others?' 'What are the qualities needed to be chair of a large company?' 'What causes nations to follow dictators and demagogues?' In the process, Psychology often takes upon itself the task of addressing issues that many would still see to be the province of other specialists. Thus, Psychology may ask the question, 'Why do people believe in God?' or 'What makes people commit crimes?' These are not only questions; they are also assertions that religious belief and criminality are susceptible to psychological explanations in ways that believers and sociologists may quarrel with.

Psychology has struggled to establish itself alongside the traditional scientific disciplines. Physicists (until recently at least) have taught us that the universe is a tangible phenomenon that is both measurable and predictable. Psychologists have yet to convince us that human behaviour is explicable in terms of physically determined and quantifiable mental states. Questions such as, 'What, then, makes us more than merely very intelligent animals?' or 'Is there such a thing as Free Will that is not psychologically explicable and predictable?' have not been answered to everyone's satisfaction – particularly not those who argue that a more powerful determinant of human behaviour is our social and physical environment. Even psychologists disagree about these matters: some would argue that, given time, their young science will be able to explain all human behaviour; others do not go so far, preferring more limited objectives. Many who are not psychologists repudiate utterly the notion that human beings can be reduced to the status of predictable and thus controllable automata.

Whatever the outcome of this debate Psychology, which already has firm links with Biology and Chemistry, cannot avoid these issues, which bring it also into the realms of religion, Philosophy, Sociology and Politics. It is not a subject for the faint-hearted. As a student of Psychology you must be prepared to encounter violently opposed views of the truth to an extent unfamiliar to many scientists; you must enjoy debate and be prepared to exercise judgement. In the process your perception of yourself and those around you is likely to be changed.

Subject criteria

AS

Knowledge of at least two of the following core areas of psychology:

- cognitive
- social
- developmental
- individual differences
- physiological

These are related to:

- theories, concepts and terminology
- ethical issues
- the scientific nature of psychology
- quantitative and qualitative methods of investigation
- understanding of the individual, social and cultural diversity

AS & A2

Select and apply theoretical knowledge to the solution of problems

Design and report investigations drawing valid conclusions

A2

Knowledge of the remainder of the core areas above not studied in AS. These are related to:

- strengths and weaknesses of research methods
- application to cultural, social and contemporary issues
- the interrelationship between different areas of psychology and different disciplines

Options

The OCR specification offers six options in A2 of which candidates choose two. The six comprise Psychology and – Education, Health, Organisations, Environment, Sport and Crime. The Edexcel specification offers A2 options in Applications of Psychology where candidates select two from Clinical, Criminal, Educational, Employment or Sports Psychology and one from Child, Environmental and Health Psychology.

Coursework

Students who follow the OCR specification carry out one psychological investigation as part of AS and submit a psychology research report as a component of A2. The investigation is assessed under exam conditions but candidates are able to use material from their practical work as an aide memoire. The research report involves a standard format psychological report of a practical project around 1200 words in length. Edexcel candidates are required to undertake one investigation as part of AS, the written report being subject to external examination.

Course information

Requirements

GCSE English at grade C or above is likely to be required; GCSE Maths at a minimum grade C will be preferred.

Goes well with

Any subject; particularly Biology, Mathematics (including Statistics).

Higher education suitability

Acceptable subject for most degree courses though a course requirement for none; degree courses that require either one or two sciences often do not count Psychology as a science, though it may be acceptable as a third A-level; accepted for admission to Psychology degrees, but many universities prefer a background in Mathematics or Biology.

Suggested reading

H. Coolican. *Introduction to Research Methods & Statistics in Psychology.* Hodder & Stoughton

R. Gross. *Psychology: The Science of Mind and Behaviour.* Hodder & Stoughton

N. Hayes. *Foundations of Psychology.* Routledge

I. Roth. *Introduction to Psychology.* Open University

RELIGIOUS STUDIES

'Religion' may be defined as the belief that there is some higher, unseen power or principle that controls and explains the existence and destiny of mankind. In most religions this unseen power is thought of as one or more gods, who must be obeyed and worshipped; so a religion will have associated with it rituals and customs and, sometimes, a whole artistic and cultural tradition. Religions generally embody a set of mental and moral attitudes, and will often dictate almost every aspect of how life should be lived.

Religion has been enormously influential in human affairs. There is evidence of religious activity in some of the very earliest known societies, and in almost all of the 'primitive' societies still in existence today. Religion has motivated people to construct spectacular buildings, to create artistic masterpieces and to fight terrible wars. The morals and politics of whole nations, such as the ancient Egyptians and Israelites, and modern Islamic states such as Pakistan and Iran, not to mention Ireland, closer to home, have been formulated on religious principles and our own society and culture have been moulded by the Christian religion (and also, perhaps by reaction to it).

One good reason for studying religion is, therefore, that it has been such a significant part of human life. Another is that religious questions are vitally important ones: we should all want to know whether, for example, there is life after death; and whether our actions are being watched by a divine being who will punish or reward us in the afterlife according to what He (or She) sees. It is certainly not necessary to be 'religious' to investigate these questions; and religion is often now studied by people who believe that there is no higher unseen power or principle at all.

The study of religion is an enormous undertaking, and is divided into many specialised academic disciplines. These include the study of 'Theology' (which means 'discussion about God'); and in the Christian tradition, 'Biblical Studies', which involve detailed study of the history and texts of the Old and New Testaments; and a great deal of academic work has been done on the history of Christianity and of the Christian Church. In the past studies of religion in British schools and universities were often restricted to the Christian tradition, but now a much wider range of topics is found in syllabuses. These include 'Comparative Religions' or 'World Religions': the study of religious traditions other than Christianity. The philosophical study of religious language and theories is also now widely taught, and here particularly the work of those who think religion is false is as widely known and discussed as the work of defenders of religion. The moral codes and principles that are recommended or demanded by religions are widely studied; and most courses also include some examination of attempts to provide a scientific analysis of religious belief and behaviour by sociologists, psychologists and anthropologists.

Subject criteria

A-level candidates should demonstrate a wider range and greater depth of knowledge of the criteria below. A greater maturity of thought and expression is expected together with more developed analytical skills.

AS & A2

Study one or more religions across one or more of the following areas:

- textual studies
- theological studies
- history of religious traditions
- religious ethics
- religious practice
- philosophy of religion
- psychology of religion
- sociology of religion

Acquire knowledge of:

- key concepts, eg religious beliefs, teachings and doctrines
- contribution of people, traditions and movements
- language and terminology

Options

The OCR specification offers three alternatives at AS, concentrating on either Philosophy of religion, Religious ethics or the selection of two complementary areas of study from a wide range of options. A-level candidates must study two complementary areas from the range available. Examples of available units include: Foundation for the study of religion (compulsory), Jewish scriptures, New Testament Gospels, New Testament: The early Church, Buddhism, Hinduism, Islam, Judaism. The AQA specification offers one compulsory and two optional units at both AS and A2. Options include the Old Testament, the New Testament, Aspects of a major world faith and Religion and science.

Coursework

OCR A2 modules are assessed both by examination and by an extended essay of 2000–2500 words, which is externally marked. Extended essay titles are set in advance by OCR. There is no coursework option in the AQA specification.

Course information

Requirements

Whilst previous qualifications in the subject are unlikely to be required, a GCSE grade A–C in English may be a prerequisite.

Goes well with

Any subject.

Higher education suitability

Particularly relevant preparation for studying Theology; however, the range of skills and concepts involved in this flexible subject make it an effective preparation for all of the humanities and many of the social sciences.

> **Suggested reading**
> J. Drane. *Introducing the Old Testament*. Lion
> J. Drane. *Introducing the New Testament*. Lion
> H. Chadwick. *The Early church*. Pelican, *History of the Church* series
>   (or any other of the volumes in this series)

SOCIOLOGY

Sociologists work on the assumption that our behaviour is wholly or largely explained by 'outside' factors – for instance by the social conditions we live in and our environment. Consider the question, 'Why are there so few women on the boards of public companies?' A biologist might frame a reply in terms of predictable consequences of physical differences; and a psychologist might focus on the incompatibility of so-called 'feminine' characteristics with a generally male world. A sociologist, on the other hand, will examine the dominance of a 'male' culture, the assumptions (shared by many men and women) that men perform some jobs better than women, and the consequences of women's traditional responsibility for child-rearing.

Sociology looks at all areas of human social behaviour. How do we learn to be good parents? What is the nature of human intelligence? Why do the inhabitants of some countries go to church more than others?

There is a Sociology of illness and of medicine. (Why are some social groups more likely to die of heart disease than others?) There is a Sociology of education. (Why do applicants from public schools obtain more than a fair share of places at Oxford and Cambridge Universities?) There is a Sociology of the family. (Why have the number of single-parent families increased in recent years?)

Sociologists frequently appear subversive to received views and to authority – hence the association with the left wing of politics; but it was not always so. Sociology began earlier this century as a defence of the status quo, and only since the Second World War has it come to fuel the argument for social change. As an academic activity it originally grew in response to the need for reliable data about the society we lived in and today one of its most significant applications is still the provision of the data on which governmental social policies depend.

Sociology is a subject much associated with controversy. Traditional sociological thinkers like to present their conclusions in scientific terms. More recently writers have challenged the assumption that the objects of sociological investigation may usefully be treated in this quasi-scientific way. Truth, they say, is more subjective: it depends on the values and presuppositions of the questioner.

Sociology is not a suitable subject for someone who likes to see everything is black and white, nor for those whose beliefs cannot tolerate questioning. Those who study the subject will learn to seek explanations to life in sociological terms; in the process they will learn how to ask the right questions, to assess evidence and present a conclusion. They will also examine the work of important sociological thinkers, and assimilate their ideas; they will learn to do so critically. This is not a subject for the intellectually lazy.

Subject criteria

The knowledge, understanding and skills required for AS and A-level are not listed separately. A greater depth and range of knowledge is expected of A-level candidates together with more highly developed skills of analysis and evaluation.

AS & A2

Study the following concepts and theoretical issues:

- social order, control and changes
- conflict and consensus
- social structure and action
- social facts
- role of values
- sociology and social policy

Methods of sociological enquiry:

- acquisition of primary and secondary data
- analysis of quantitative and qualitative data
- design and execution of sociological research
- ethical issues of sociological research

Socialisation, culture and identity

Social differentiation, power and stratification

Identify and evaluate significant sociological trends

Awareness of theoretical debates in Sociology

Options

The OCR specification offers numerous options across several modules, these include: Family, Mass media, Religion, Youth and culture, Crime and deviance, Education, Social policy and welfare. The AQA specification offers two units at AS each with three options, eg Unit 1 has alternatives of Family and households, Health and mass media. Further options are available in two of the A2 units.

Coursework

In the OCR AS specification coursework is optional and consists of a report on a short piece of sociological research. The research could be studies carried out by the candidate or professional sociological research. In A2 coursework is offered as an optional personal study of the candidate's choice drawn from any

part of the specification and 2000–2500 words in length. AQA coursework is
optional in both AS and A2. AS coursework covers sociological methods and
their relationship to theory; additionally A2 coursework covers issues such as
Values and objectivity and Post-modernity. Coursework in AS comprises a
research proposal of less than 1200 words; the A2 component is a sociological
study with a maximum of 3500 words.

Course information

Requirements
GCSE Sociology is not normally required; GCSE English at grade C or above
is likely to be.

Goes well with
Any subject.

Higher education suitability
A valid and acceptable academic A-level for university entrance purposes;
good preparation for degree courses in the social sciences, though not a
prerequisite for studying Sociology at university.

Suggested reading
T. Bilton et al. *Introductory Sociology.* Macmillan
M. Haralambos & M. Holborn. *Sociology: Themes & Perspectives.* Collins
R. Jenkins. *Social Identity.* Routledge
T. Lawson. *Sociology for A Level: A Skills-based Approach.* Collins

The Trotman Web Site

The Trotman Publishing Web Site has been developed for all those interested in careers and higher education.

Each address has its own distinct function, and all are accessible from the Trotman Publishing home page (www.trotmanpublishing.co.uk).
Bookmark these sites and benefit from using our online services.

www.trotmanpublishing.co.uk
All our company information at the click of a mouse button

- **Publication dates** – know what is coming and when
- **Read reviews of books** – what other people have said about them
- *Win Your Rent* online entry
- **Contact us** – give us your feedback
- **Special offers** – take advantage of seasonal offers

www.careers-portal.co.uk
A links portal site dedicated to careers guidance

- 1,700 links in an easy-to-use search format
- Use the search facility to locate sites by subject
- Voted by The Daily Mail one of the Top Ten careers sites

www.careersuk.co.uk
The UK's only online e-commerce bookstore dedicated to careers

- Over 300 careers-related book and CD-ROM titles
- Fast database interrogation allows searches by title, author, subject or ISBN
- Order directly over the internet using our secure credit card facility

So whatever you want to know about careers resources, news or organisations, it's available online from

Trotman